YOU'RE NOT PARANOID: THE ESSENTIAL CONSPIRACY THRILLERS

Stephen Hoover

You're Not Paranoid: The Essential Conspiracy Thrillers

Library of Congress Control Number: 2014909507

Copyright © 2013 by Stephen Hoover

Book design by: Cat Stewart

Cover design by: 2Faced Design

ISBN: 978-1-941084-20-5

Dedicated to Dr. Jeff Demouy, for suggesting the title and buying the popcorn.

Table of Contents

Intro

Paranoid thrillers provide an interesting group of films to examine. They oftentimes reflect the anxieties of the time very well. Given the amount of conspiracy theories out there, there are plenty of directions in which writers can go with this type of material.

A good paranoid thriller usually has a standard structure, which is explored in the chapters that follow. The real complexity in these tales is oftentimes found in the labyrinthine nature of the conspiracies themselves. Part of the fun in these films—or the fear—is almost always watching the protagonist peel back the layers of the conspiracy, getting closer to the truth, and danger, as they do.

There's more to these films than thrills, however. Some of them provide a great deal of commentary on real life events. Some of them are firmly based in real life events. Others are both, based on real life events, but tending to give credence to particular conspiracy theories surrounding those events. It's up to the viewer to decide what's real and what's just paranoid.

You'll find very intelligent films among those featured in the second section of this book. That second section contains spoilers, so you may well want to watch the films first and then refer to the second section for clarification or interpretation of some of the films' major story points. Most of the films in this book will appeal to people who like intelligent, mystery-driven stories and action-driven stories alike, which is one of the best things about these types of films.

Get ready for some rather intense, intellectually challenging and memorable films!

Chapter 1

Discovering the Truth

Questioning one's sanity, discovering a horrible and hidden truth and surviving the fallout: these are all the hallmarks of paranoia thrillers. Paranoia thrillers have remained popular for decades, with the 1970s seeing such films produced in great number. Most of these films center on the protagonist unraveling a vast conspiracy, and those conspiracy theories oftentimes mirror ones that actually existed—or exist—in real life.

Not all conspiracy theories turn out to be the ramblings of paranoid individuals. In recent years, government and corporate spying, fake intelligence and other scandals have confirmed some of the worst fears—or, it seems, greatest hopes—of conspiracy theorists.

In many cases, fiction provides a safe way to explore parts of life that are, in fact, quite threatening. Horror allows us to experience terror without risk. Even romantic comedies allow us to experience the ups and downs of love without any emotional hazard. Paranoid thrillers allow us to discover deeply and deliberately buried secrets without risking our own safety, and allow us to thrill as the protagonists put it all on the line to expose the truth.

Some of the films you'll find in this book, such as *The Insider* and *Silkwood,* are based on real life incidents where information that should have been made public was allegedly buried deliberately. Others, such as *Conspiracy Theory*, are entirely fictional, but play on conspiracy theories that have taken on a life of their own in our broader culture, becoming legends that endure over decades. Either way, these films provide some of the best examples of thrillers, and are oftentimes quite dark, but not always.

What Makes Them Work

We'll take an in-depth look at why these thrillers tend to work so well as we go through the films, but there are some aspects of conspiracy theories that make them fertile grounds for paranoid thriller writers. When one considers how the typical conspiracy theory works, it's not hard to understand why Hollywood has found them to be such desirable foundations for great paranoid thrillers.

In the film *Conspiracy Theory*, Mel Gibson's character makes a revealing comment about conspiracy theories. If you can prove them, they're really not good conspiracy theories.

This is, in fact, true. Conspiracy theories are built on mystery and the unknown. They almost always involve an organization that's accountable for some great evil, whether that organization is a cabal of elite, power-hungry cultists like the Illuminati or a product of a more rational age, such as a government intelligence agency. No matter where the conspiracy is hatched, however, if the group doing the conspiring can be identified and proven to be attached to the conspiracy, it's no longer a conspiracy theory. It becomes a fact and, in some cases, a criminal case.

These theories oftentimes seem to mirror real life events, as do the films that come out during the times when those conspiracies become most popular. During the 1970s, as we'll see in the section on the films, there was a great interest in films that depicted government conspiracies that involved covering up embarrassing incidents, getting more control over the machinations of government or government officials trying to avoid being held accountable for their actions. This, of course, mirrors what went on during the Watergate scandal, a criminal conspiracy that reached the highest levels of power and that had frightening implications for the nation as a whole.

While such films oftentimes follow a protagonist who manages to expose some kind of corruption in government, sometimes with hopeful results, other paranoid thrillers center on conspiracies and organizations that simply cannot be held accountable.

Many Different Culprits

In some of these films, we'll see conspiracies made up of entities that are either wholly unaccountable or far too powerful to be held accountable at all. In *They Live* for instance, not only is the conspiring antagonist organization unaccountable, it's not even earthly. In *Marathon Man*, the paranoia is driven by a group of people who exist underground but who wield very real power and who are not afraid to torture and kill to protect their interests: ex-Nazis.

These types of conspiracy theories can unfold in many different ways. In some cases, a sympathetic worker or agent for a government agency will want to help the protagonist, but the protagonist will have to convince that person that they're not just paranoid. In other cases, the government may be found to be conspiring with the conspirators themselves, raising frightening questions regarding who can be trusted and how far.

A third type of conspirator has become very popular in recent years—corporations. They can exist simultaneously above and below the waters, providing an incredible level of threat to the protagonist.

The Corporate Conspiracy

People have absolutely no trouble believing that dark and callous forces will conspire to make a profit off of innocent people, no matter what the cost. The film *Coma*, featured in this book, involves a sinister plot involving organ theft, with doctors and corporations betraying the people who entrust them with their lives. An urban legend holds that the film reduced the number of people willing to donate organs, though this is of debatable veracity.

The Insider and *The Constant Gardener* both play on corporate conspiracy theories and are very effective. These films may be dramatized or outright fictionalized, but they're certainly not entirely fictional. Corporate conspiracies, from manipulating energy prices to hiding the known dangers of automobiles, are established facts, and they're frightening in their implications.

A corporate conspiracy can oftentimes bring into play the amount of control these organizations wield over government power and, when they do, things can get very frightening very quickly.

The Nature of the Fear

Rational people avoid assumptions. Simply because a corporation is found to have been engaged in some sort of conspiracy involving profit or power doesn't mean that all corporations are engaged in such behavior. Then again, maybe it does.

This is almost always what really drives the tension in these films. Is the protagonist paranoid and slipping further and further into it or are they on to something? Are they paranoid because of some delusional disorder or are they paranoid because everyone really is out to get them?

In order for these films to work, we have to have a protagonist who, at some level, doubts themselves. This allows the audience to be convinced by the evidence, just as the protagonist gradually is and, as we find out the truth along with the protagonist, things get frightening.

Understanding Why It's So Frightening

As you go through the following chapters on the films, keep something in mind. These films almost always deal with a breach of trust, a betrayal of some sort. If the government is at the heart of the conspiracy, it's the betrayal of the concepts of accountability and fairness that are at the heart of democratic and representative forms of government. The conspiracy is avoiding the system so that they consolidate power, in some cases, or simply assuming that the normal checks and balances shouldn't apply to them in others. This is terrifying at its root as it means that the entire system is just a sham and the nation is really just an oligarchy or even a fascist state posing as a democracy.

In other cases, we have corporations behind the conspiracies, which is equally frightening. Cynical notions aside, corporations embody the promise of capitalism. A good idea, combined with hard work, can enable the people who found corporations to become enormously wealthy and successful. When the corporations subvert the law and start stealing and killing to make a buck, they threaten not only their victims, but the entire notion that the system is fair and that it rewards hard work. In these films, the implication is that the system is based on rewarding wealth with power and on the connections the people at the top have rather than them deserving to enjoy the positions that they do.

These are frightening concepts and they play into what all conspiracy theories imply at some level. The system is rigged, reality is a lie and, were you to really figure out who and what are responsible for the wickedness in the world, *they* would probably make sure you disappeared, or destroy your credibility to the point that you couldn't get a single rational person to listen to you.

It's a nightmare. Like any serious nightmare, it's sometimes hard to tell the difference between when one is awake and when one is asleep.

Doubt, Paranoia and Power
As you go through these films, imagine yourself in the place of the protagonist. You find out something that implies that not only has a government or corporation been lying, but that those lies go so far and so deep that just about everything people believe is simply not true. How do you tell someone about that? How do you prove it? How do you hold anyone accountable? Even more, how do you know that it's not *you* who has the problem here?

You can see people who have fallen far into paranoia everywhere. They have Internet shows, call into late night AM radio programs, publish newsletters and walk around the streets carrying signs that accuse the government or corporations of heinous crimes that extend over years, decades and sometimes even centuries. These people are generally regarded as embodying some type of paranoia, but what if they're right? What if the government raised a false flag to start every war? What if the corporations are poisoning our water and food to make a profit? What if the fluoride in the water is there not to strengthen your teeth—that's what it's there for, we're just speculating here—but to make you more subject to mind control?

These movies are all about what if questions and how we go about addressing them as rational people. It's about what we, thinking, intelligent people would do if we came across a situation that undeniably proved that there was some sort of a conspiracy going on and we had to deal with the fallout of that.

We could become a whistleblower, having to run off to another country to seek protection from the forces we exposed in our own. We could end up being the victim of a murder, as the protagonist in *Silkwood* is implied to be in the film. We could have our lives destroyed, our reputations ruined, our families humiliated and harassed or we could just end up disappeared somewhere, with no one knowing where we are or what happened to us.

We could also end up in a dentist's chair having our teeth drilled as a form of torture, being asked questions to which there's no answer that would satisfy the interrogator.

These are all terrifying scenarios, and they make paranoia thrillers incredibly engaging. These films all ask that one question we'd want answered if we discovered something as frightening, expansive and dangerous as a high-level conspiracy: Is it safe?

What to Expect

These films are oftentimes complex, engaging and full of twists and turns. They employ the techniques of crime, military, mystery and other types of thrillers to keep the viewer's interest.

Among these films, you'll find some of the most intelligent storytelling in any genre. These are thrillers made for adults. They oftentimes have some very action-packed sequences during their runtimes, but these aren't pure action films. They oftentimes have elements of a police procedural, but no clear good guys and bad guys, at least where the authorities are concerned.

These are stories of outsiders who get a glimpse into secret societies, organizations, the smoky backrooms where politicians and the captains of industry collude and, sometimes, where they see genuine threats from other planets. Would you believe them if they told you what they'd seen? Probably not, and that's where the paranoia comes into play.

Expect to see a lot of characters wrestling with their own sanity. Expect to see a lot of characters going through a great deal of pain as what they normally would have suspected was a fantasy is proven to be a very frightening reality.

Most of all, expect these movies to stick with you more than most. The stories are oftentimes incredibly memorable. Perhaps because they do so often mirror what happens in real life, they resonate in a way that few stories do.

You may even find yourself looking up the conspiracies that are featured in the films, or the ones that the film is based on. This can make for some engaging research and, some day, you might just find yourself calling into an AM radio show and wondering if someone listening has decided that you know too much.

After all, just because you're paranoid doesn't mean they're not out to get you!

Chapter 2

The Paranoia Primer: The Theories and the Films

You'll find that many of the films in the second section of this book are based primarily on real-life conspiracy theories. If they don't reference those conspiracy theories directly, they'll substitute an invented conspiracy theory—and usually an invented antagonist organization—for the film's purposes.

Understanding some of the basics of the conspiracy theories that these films use to motivate the action is helpful. Here are some of the biggest. These are only overviews of these theories. There are many different variations on any one of them. The Internet is full of pages on these various theories, but here are the big ones that you're going to run into in these films, and the basics of what they say.

Nazi War Criminals and their Networks

Some of these films have plots that revolve around the protagonist discovering a network of Nazi war criminals on the run. Many Nazi war criminals did flee to South America following the end of the war, evading capture. In fact, as of 2013, the Jewish Virtual Library lists several former Nazis who are still believed to be alive and in hiding.

This is among the few conspiracies in these films that are provable beyond a shadow of a doubt. Some of the most wanted members of the Third Reich did manage to survive the end of the war and to stay beyond the reach of authorities. They include very well-known figures such as Josef Mengele, who died in Brazil, never being caught or tried for his crimes. He, in fact, is the central Nazi figure in the film *The Boys from Brazil.*

The Archetype

In films featuring escaped Nazis, expect them to be wealthy, powerful and feared. Also expect them to be supported by a network of followers or, at least, private muscle. In some films, the organizations that these individuals belong to will still be carrying out missions. In others, the characters will simply be trying to evade being captured and tried for their crimes.

The archetypical escaped Nazi will usually be completely unrepentant for their crimes and, in fact, will likely be committing more crimes along the lines of those for which they are infamous. Mengele will still be conducting bizarre medical experiments, for instance. The lower level officers and killers will still be killing on the orders of their superiors.

The escaped Nazi may or may not have contacts in existing governments that keep them safe. A common motivation for this is either the tremendous wealth that the Nazi commands or the fact that the escaped Nazi still has followers devoted to their original beliefs. The escaped Nazi may also have saved their own skin by turning in their comrades in exchange for not being captured themselves.

There are still organizations actively pursuing these individuals, some of whom are now well into their 90s. Recent changes in how charges need to be brought against known Nazi war criminals may make it easier to bring them to trial when their whereabouts are known.

In films based on post-World War II Nazi conspiracies, there is a truth that most of the plots are built on. These individuals remained beyond the reach of the law, and some are still out there.

UFOs and Aliens

UFO and alien conspiracies usually hold to one or more points:

o Extraterrestrial aliens have been to or are on Earth.

o Government agencies are aware of this.

o The aliens' plans are likely malicious.

The government will go to any length to cover it up, if they know.

Just about any film that deals with extraterrestrials will have one of these elements at the core of its plot. Oftentimes, the aliens are actually in power in some regard. They may collude with or even run certain sections of the government. They may have infiltrated the local police force. They may even run huge corporations. It's usually implied that, in addition to whatever power they have as a result of their advanced technology, they also have the advantage of vast, Earth-based power structures being at their beck and call.

Films such as *The Arrival* and *They Live* play into the basics of this conspiracy. Both involve aliens who have come to Earth and who wield tremendous amounts of power. They have connections to Earth-based power brokers, but, when needed, they can call in their own resources to silence someone trying to let the truth be known.

To make sure that the sinister extraterrestrial aims can be carried out in secret, the aliens will oftentimes camouflage themselves as human beings. An alternative explanation for their being able to remain hidden is erasing people's memories or using government agents—or assassins—to eliminate problem individuals.

There are many, many different variations on the basic alien conspiracy theory. These conspiracy theories, perhaps because they're not always politically charged, seem to have a lot of mainstream popularity. The television show *Ancient Aliens* is built on trying to connect events in Earth history to some sort of alien presence.

The Archetype
The archetypical alien conspiracy in films involves a race of aliens that want to exploit the planet, humanity or both, usually with the goal of completely controlling it in the end. They might be taking over power structures and planting their own agents high up in them. They may be behind a transition to a bland, consumer society that lives only to breed and obey. They may try to trash the entire planet's ecosystem, making it more like their own planet and driving homo sapiens to extinction.

In practice, the aliens will operate much like a government agency. They'll cover up information, destroy the reputations of people who threaten them, kill people when they have to and remain completely behind the scenes the whole time. In some cases, they'll rely on the fact that someone claiming that the world has been taken over by aliens sounds completely mad and that they're unlikely to ever be believed.

Assassination Conspiracies
Paranoid thrillers that involve plots to assassinate dangerous individuals tend to follow a particular set of conventions. They oftentimes mirror JFK assassination conspiracies if the plot uses conspirators invented for the sake of the film, such as *The Parallax View*. In other cases, such as in *JFK*, the films may be based on or even advocate for a particular conspiracy theory constructed around a real-life event.

Paranoid thrillers based on assassinations usually have as their central theme that the public is being deceived about the identity and motivation of a killer who assassinated a figure who was dangerous to the existing order. Maverick politicians are favored victims in these stories.

Alternately, the plot may revolve around an assassination that has yet to happen and the tension in the film is generated by following the protagonists as they try to stop it from happening at all. Either way, there will be some collection of shady interests behind the assassination, usually the military-industrial complex, however it is represented in any given film.

The Archetype
The archetype for this type of conspiracy involves clandestine intelligence organizations, military, and ideological organizations all working together to kill off an inconvenient political figure. This is, essentially, what Garrison in *JFK* discovers. This is also what characters in several other films discover.

The group ordering the killing will oftentimes be aided and abetted by the government. The very beginning of *The Parallax View* shows us a high bench from which a Senate committee announces that a recent political assassination was the work of one crazed man. That man will be the patsy. The protagonist will find out whom the real killer is, usually with a contact within the clandestine intelligence community providing a massive information dump at some point. While information dumps usually come off as contrived and are boring to watch, in the hands of a master filmmaker such as Oliver Stone they can go on for 15 minutes or more and be utterly captivating.

These films will oftentimes follow along the lines of any one of a number of real-life conspiracy theories. If the film involves the JFK assassination, there are seemingly endless culprits to implicate and endless connections that can be made between them.

Look for a protagonist to be in more danger as they get closer to the truth. This might manifest as threats against their family and their reputations or attempts on their life.

The Government or Corporate Cover-up
The government has done something embarrassing or illegal. Whichever organizations within the government are involved want to keep anyone from finding out, and woe to anyone who does. There may also be a corporation at the center of this type of conspiracy, such as is the case in *The Constant Gardener.*

In these films, the forces maintaining the cover-up may be rogue forces within the government who are striking it out on their own, such as in *Conspiracy Theory*. They may also be official parts of the government, such as in *JFK*, where it's implied that the conspiracy goes to the very highest levels.

There are endless theories involving government and corporate cover-ups. They range from sinister seeming programs such as HAARP—which really isn't that sinister—to anti-vaccination conspiracy theories. These are not all far-fetched and, of course, there have been real instances where companies and/or governments have conspired to keep embarrassing or damaging information out of the public sphere.

The Archetype
Don't be surprised to see government and corporations working together to maintain a cover-up in these films. Oftentimes, it's implied that the interests of the government and whatever corporation is involved are so closely related that there's virtually no difference between the two organizations, weapons manufacturers and the military in *JFK*, for instance.

Many of these films—most all of them, in fact—involve a cover-up of one sort or another. This plotline oftentimes flows from the first. An assassination or alien invasion, for instance, leads to a conspiracy to cover evidence up and eliminate anyone who knows. *Capricorn One* is one of the films in this book that are very much dominated by a massive cover-up.

The Moon Landing Hoax
The alleged hoaxing of the moon landings is technically another cover-up conspiracy theory, but it plays a large enough role in one of the films featured in this book that it deserves its own section.

These theories all generally hold that NASA faked the moon landings, for a variety of different reasons. Different methods of hoaxing the moon landing are also described by various conspiracy theorists.

The evidence given to back up these conspiracy theories mostly consists of photo analyses of the pictures of the astronauts on the moon. The theories, in plain language, are oftentimes based on poor understandings of optics, physics and photography.

For example, the planting of the American flag by Neil Armstrong and Buzz Aldrin on their first trip to the moon is one of the most often forwarded pieces of "evidence" for this theory. The typical claim is that the way that the flag moves indicates that there is wind. This is easily debunked and only shows that the claimant doesn't really know much about the equipment brought to the moon with the astronauts.

Most of the claims are along these lines, but they make for a great story. Essentially, the story goes that NASA filmed all of the footage that was supposed to have come from the moon in a studio. The movement of the astronauts, the lighting, the behavior of the lunar soil near the landing craft and other features of the photographs and footage are oftentimes pointed to by conspiracy theorists as evidence of a hoax.

This all can make for a great story. What if it were true? How far would NASA and the government go to cover it up? If you're a paranoid thriller writer, all the way, of course.

In fact, keep that in mind for all of these various types of conspiracies. What makes them truly threatening is that the people behind them will do anything to cover them up, no matter what the conspiracy may be about!

Chapter 3

The Sinister Agents of the Conspiracy

In these films, the actual antagonist is oftentimes something rather intangible. It might be a secret group of powerful people, a corporation or an alliance of corporations or something else made up of people, but that's also intensely impersonal. To give life to the conspiracy, there has to be some kind of physical antagonist that can pose a real threat to the protagonist character.

Enter the agents of the conspiracy. They come in many forms and can be used creatively to symbolize the entire conspiracy and what it really stands for.

Intelligence Agents

Intelligence agents are used here as an umbrella term for the shady, deadly characters that oftentimes directly pursue the protagonist. They may be from the CIA, the DOD, the FBI, the NSA or a variety of other real or fictional agencies. In some cases, the agencies that they work for have more cryptic names, such as "The Division".

These agents are typically very dangerous. In some films, such as *Capricorn One*, they consist of military personnel, federal agents and other actual government employees who are working on top-secret projects. In films such as *Marathon Man*, it's not entirely clear whom the intelligence agents work for. They're about as slippery as they come.

The intelligence agents sometimes shadow the main characters. If they're good, they'll do it in a way that frightens the protagonist, but that also makes the protagonist wonder if they're just being paranoid. The intelligence agents sometimes function as assassins or sometimes serve other roles. In some films, for instance, government agents destroy the reputations of agitators by framing them for crimes or just harassing and cajoling them.

A conspiracy-specific variation on this comes in the form of the men in black. These agents are usually portrayed as being part of a UFO cover-up. They generally function to silence people. Sometimes they're described as having telepathic or other powers and may be aliens themselves. The men in black, however, are usually described as looking like stereotypical secret agents or CIA spooks. The conspiracies they're usually associated with almost always involve shutting down the public's access to information about UFOs.

While these agents can be major threats, they can also be great resources.

The Turncoat Agent
A turncoat agent is a sort of a deep throat character that feeds

information to the protagonist. These are ambiguous characters, as they may simply be giving the protagonist disinformation as a way of throwing them off their task.

The turncoat agent, however, can sometimes be a very memorable character. There were several of these characters in the television show *The X-Files* throughout its run, with the infamous Smoking Man at times playing this role.

The turncoat agent has an incredible amount of information to share. He or she functions as a way to clear up what's not clear to the viewers and to send the protagonist on toward success. See *JFK* for one of the best sequences of all featuring an agent betraying a conspiracy and giving up all the information the protagonist needs.

Corporate Conspiracy Thugs

Corporate conspiracy thugs can be anyone. They might be high-ranking government officials who have a financial interest in the corporation or they might be military governments that want to keep up relations with the corporation to enrich a dictator and his lackeys. You'll see this sort of character pop up in many roles. In some cases, they provide the muscle for the corporation and, in others, they identify troublemakers.

In a scene in *The Constant Gardener*, for instance, one of the main characters and an associate accost a high-ranking African government official at a party. They ask him a series of loaded questions about disappearing drugs, if the drugs were directly converted into his fancy car and so forth. He's a thug of the conspiracy, but a high-ranking one. He's not going to kill anyone himself but you can be sure that, if he finds out you're a threat, he's going to pass that information along.

Companies might hire thugs to do their dirty work. In the same film, the main characters have run-ins with heavies that work for the pharma company at the center of the film's conspiracy.

In films such as *Coma*, the corporate conspiracy sometimes involves several different companies all working in tandem. In that film, a hospital is providing much needed medical products and auctions them off to the highest bidder. Any of those bidders have to know that what they're doing is illegal and, of course, they must also know that murder is involved. In the film, the conspiracy goes all the way to the top of one of the most prestigious hospitals in Boston, with another institute being in on it as well, and people throughout both companies being part of the plot.

Because corporate types are involved, goons are usually used to pursue the protagonists. In some cases, however, there may be several levels of harassment involved. In *The Insider*, a whistleblower is subjected to harassment of many different kinds by a tobacco company that wants to avoid being held liable for the dangerous nature of the products that they sell.

Whether they're using threats, beat downs or outright murder, corporate thugs are among the most frightening characters in these films. Because they're not part of any intelligence agency, there's the presumption that they're mercenaries of a sort and are oftentimes willing to go all the way to killing to make a buck defending the secrets of their corporate masters.

Any corporation can be involved in such activities, but keep a careful eye out in these films for energy and pharmaceutical companies. The military-industrial complex conspirators implicated in films such as *JFK*, of course, imply a union between the worst that the government and private industry have to offer, which is doubly frightening.

The Destroyer of Reputations

Before a company or a government moves up to outright murder, they oftentimes try to destroy the reputations of the people exposing their secrets. This happens in films ranging from *JFK* to *The Arrival* to *Mercury Rising.* These operators are usually implied to be working behind the scenes.

In *JFK*, Garrison is publically accused of drugging his witnesses, which, according to the film's narrative, was a lie. He's also accused of going after the defendant in his case because the defendant happens to be homosexual.

The person exposing the conspiracy theory will oftentimes have their professional reputation destroyed. This happens to the protagonist in *The Arrival*, who finds out that he's been let go from his job and that he's not likely to get hired by anyone else. In *Mercury Rising*, the protagonist finds himself being pursued as a kidnapper, which he technically is, though he's kidnapped a child to protect that child from a crooked NSA agent who wants him dead.

Somewhere within the conspiracy is a master of media whose sole purpose is to destroy the reputations of those who are inconvenient to whatever interests they work for. Oftentimes, before the worst of the persecution starts for the person who discovered the conspiracy and before we see them running for their lives, we'll see them simply trying to keep their professional and personal reputations intact as forces beyond their control start to tear them apart.

This is almost guaranteed to happen in most of these films, so keep an eye out for it in the story arcs!

Chapter 4

The Investigation Arc

Like many films in the thriller genre, those that rely on paranoia to motivate their characters oftentimes have complex plots. The best of these films don't assume that the audience knows anything in particular about the conspiracy. Part of the action involves us following the protagonist and they discover the truth of whatever's going on in the film's universe or, in cases where the films are based on real life, on their real investigations.

The investigation arc will usually take up parts of the first and second acts of these films. The confrontation with the force at the core of the conspiracy will be the climax. The time the film gives us to learn about the conspiracy can make or break it entirely and determine whether we even care about who's behind the conspiracy in the end.

The Protagonist

Fish-out-of-water characters work very well for these stories. *The Arrival, They Live, Marathon Man* and many others depend upon this type of character. This character gives us someone to identify with. Like them, we wouldn't really understand the breadth or depth of what we'd discovered in the beginning and would likely be shocked as we learned more about it. This type of protagonist is also easily put in danger, as they generally won't have any skills that make them well suited to take on a conspiracy.

In other instances, however, the protagonist is an expert and part of the movie's thrills are provided by watching them do what they do best. *The Boys from Brazil* uses such a character in the form of Ezra, a tenacious, fearless and very successful Nazi hunter. *JFK* gives us a skilled, intelligent and endlessly curious DA with a commitment to the truth to follow.

Either way, the character ought to be in over their head at some point. At some point during the film, it should become apparent to them that the tendrils of the conspiracy they've discovered reach into very high places. They should be aware that, as far as the people behind it are concerned, their life likely doesn't count for much and is easily ended.

The protagonist is sometimes skeptical and sometimes wholly accepting of there being a conspiracy. In *The Parallax View*, the protagonist is sure he's on to something. To balance out his zeal, his editor provides a more grounded character to ask the questions the audience may themselves be asking.

The protagonist, however, can be skilled and knowledgeable in some cases, but will usually become an enemy of the very agencies they work for when they start resisting or exposing the conspiracy.

The Protagonist's Helper/The Captive Woman

In more than one of the films featured in the second section of this book, you'll see a character, usually female, who ends up being coerced into spending time with the protagonist. Sometimes, the protagonist will not be friendly to them, going so far as to carjack them, invade their house, hold them at gunpoint, imprison them and so forth. Eventually, this secondary character will usually come to be an ally of the protagonist, sometimes even a lover.

While it's not featured in this book, the 2005 film *V for Vendetta* has a great example of such a character in Evey. She's brutalized and lied to by the protagonist, but eventually comes to see that there was purpose to his brutality and risks herself to help him out.

In *Three Days of the Condor* we see a character like this in Kathy, who endures being held at gunpoint, being physically restrained, car theft, threats and worse and still ends up thinking that the protagonist is a nice guy. In *Mercury Rising,* the female secondary character is not treated so brutally, but she ends up being lied to and having her life put at risk because of those lies.

In some cases, the apparent sympathizer may turn out to be a threat in and of herself—or a conspirator—and this is a popular character in these films. Keep an eye out for her, because she's also sometimes a stand-in for the audience. As the protagonist convinces her—or, rarely, him—of the truth that he's trying to expose, the audience is persuaded as well.

The Investigation

The protagonist will usually get some indication that something is amiss. They may see information released by the government or a company that goes against what they know to be true.

They may see an historical event analyzed too quickly and all dissenting opinions dismissed. They may see evidence of tampering in an investigation, the intimidation of witnesses to a major event or other signs that something is very wrong.

They may also get involved because of the cover-up already in progress. Usually, this is because characters that know something about the conspiracy—that know *too much,* in other words—start getting killed. The killings will usually be murky in and of themselves. Healthy people will have heart attacks; minor surgeries will result in comas and so forth. Somehow, someone will be taken out of the action and how it happens won't make any sense, unless someone ordered a deliberate hit and covered it up.

Ratcheting Up the Tension

During the investigation phase in these films, the tension usually increases exponentially. Some tropes are used to show the protagonist in increasing levels of danger.

It oftentimes starts with the protagonist being followed, or with the appearance of them being followed. This is a great time for the writers to inject some ambiguity. Is the protagonist being followed, or are they just getting paranoid? Of course, it's usually both.

There are oftentimes more murders on tap when the investigation gets going, as well. Quite often, as the protagonist gets closer and closer, the people close to them will start getting bumped off. *The Parallax View* and *Capricorn One* both use this method of increasing the tension as the investigation moves forward.

About that Information Dump

In many of these films, one of the most important moments is when a character that is either introduced late in the game or a character that's already established fills in the holes for the protagonist. None of the films listed in this book fail in this regard and it's vital for the success of the film.

The audience, usually by the time this moment comes along, has been watching the film for a long time. They've gone through many twists and turns, had information denied and then revealed to them and watched with the promise that, if they stuck with it, the audience would be rewarded with something stellar. If this moment appears in the story and it doesn't work the entire film is basically a waste.

To do this right, the filmmakers have to give us a theory that makes sense given what we know up until this point. It has to incorporate all or most of the players the protagonist has discovered. It has to hint that the conspiracy goes further than the protagonist imagined. The information dump should also imply that there is great danger in going forward with the investigation, which gives us an excuse to be more engaged with the protagonist as they keep on investigating.

The information dump oftentimes comes from someone who has become disgusted with the organization with whom they work and who decides to go rogue. It might be a disaffected intelligence agent or a former worker at a company who knows something that their higher ups don't want revealed. In some cases, there might be a twist.

The information dump may also come from a double agent. It may come from someone who has set themselves up as an ally and who gives up the information to gain the protagonist's trust, only to betray them.

These films thrive on characters that are ambiguous, so this is always a good move on the part of the filmmaker if they pull it off right. Given that the information giving character may be betraying their former employer by giving up the information, the audience is primed to accept that they may be lying about the whole thing as well.

This is a vital part of the process of discovering the conspiracy. It's also a great time compression technique, as potentially hours of narrative can be compressed into one monologue that puts the final touches on the film's reveal of the conspiracy.

One clever variation on this is to have the protagonist gain access to the conspirator's secret headquarters or, at least, one of their installations. This is particularly popular with paranoia thrillers involving aliens, as it allows the filmmakers to reveal the entire plot and show off some fancy alien technology at the same time.

The Chase

Unless the film is more sober, like *JFK*, paranoid thrillers oftentimes involve some sort of a chase after the secret is discovered or, at least, in the final phases of the investigation. It might be the protagonist escaping the hitmen working for the conspiracy or it might be a race to make information public before the conspirators have a chance kill off the messenger or destroy the evidence. No matter how it unfolds, this has to be one of the most engaging parts of the film, particularly if the film is very action oriented.

Ideally, the hero should be unprepared for the chase, though this can vary in some films, particularly if it's an action film. In *The Green Zone*, for instance, the protagonist is no slouch when it comes to fighting, but he's outmatched by the organization and individuals that he's up against. This allows the protagonist to have some heroic moments but to still be at risk of being killed at any time, keeping the tension high.

Chases can be slow burns or fast action sequences, either works. The tension may come about because the protagonist is being dismantled publically in terms of their reputation and credibility, because the danger to their family increases due to more threats or because they literally have someone chasing them down and have to make a desperate run for their lives.

The Reveal or Cover-up

Some of these films are quite optimistic overall, others are most certainly not. Which one applies usually comes down to the ending. Sometimes, the entire conspiracy is revealed and it's implied that people can do something to change the situation. In other films, the entire story ends up being about the futility of fighting against vast conspiracies, with the evidence buried, those involved caught or killed and the public remaining unaware that anything at all has happened.

One of the most nihilistic of endings to these films is when the protagonist actually gives their lives trying to uncover the conspiracy, to no avail. Some films, such as *Marathon Man*, dare to be a bit ambiguous as to what their endings really mean for the protagonist and are oftentimes better films for taking that risk.

If these films don't have a suitable ending, the entire affair is a waste of time. The films that people tend to remember and tend to love are those that pay off the substantial investments of time and attention required to follow some of these films and that pay it off with a great final act. Whether it's optimistic or pessimistic really isn't important as long as it's good.

The Impact

It makes sense to imply that there's some sort of impact as a result of what the protagonists find out. In *Conspiracy Theory*, the rather happy ending implies that the sinister organization behind the film's many plot points will be outed eventually by agents of another security organization dedicated to keeping everyone on the up and up. In other films, however, such as *The Parallax View,* the implication is that the system is able to keep on with its corruption and the impact of the protagonist's investigation, unfortunately, is ultimately to cement the power of the sinister organization behind the plot in the first place.

Some films go beyond the screen in their impact. In the entry on *JFK* in the next section of this book, for instance, you'll find out that the film had a tremendous real world impact on the release of records related to the assassination and on piquing people's interest in the assassination in general.

Other films, such as *The Constant Gardener* and *The Insider,* not only speak to the types of suspicions that people hold about very powerful organizations, but can sometimes help to reveal facts about those organizations and how they go about their business that may strongly influence public perception.

Paranoid thrillers, when they're based on real life events, can matter more than most other types of films and can really make a significant difference in the world, as you'll see in the cases of some of the films featured in the upcoming second section of this book.

Chapter 5

The Changing Tone of the Films

Any film will reflect the time in which it is made. This is usually—and perhaps unfortunately—most easily demonstrated in how violence is depicted in the films. The newer the film, the more violent it will likely be. There are ways that paranoid thrillers have changed over the years, however, and that are wroth pointing out, as it helps to understand the films featured in the second section of this book.

Understanding Tone
The easiest way to describe tone is simply to say that it is how the movie makes you feel. An action film should feel exciting through and through. A horror film should be dominated by a sense of dread at every turn. If the tone is right in such a film, you'll probably watch a lot of it through the spaces between your fingers as you hold your hand up to partially cover your eyes.

Tone means everything in these films, but it can vary tremendously from film to film. From the overbearing menace of *The Parallax View* to the dark comedy of *Conspiracy Theory* to the creepy, dangerous feel of *Coma*, these films embody many different feelings among them. Over the years, however, they have changed en masse in some regards, which is interesting to consider.

The 1970s: Watergate, Government Lies and Conspiracy Theories

On June 17, 1972, a group of burglars was arrested at the Democratic Party's national headquarters. That headquarters was located at the Watergate office building, from which the resulting scandal takes its name. It would eventually become so notorious that most other political scandals would be described with a name that had "gate" added to the end.

The burglars were working with the blessing of President Nixon. His goals and methods will be familiar to any fan of conspiracy thrillers.

The idea was to get information that could discredit and destroy any of his political opponents. By the time it was over, 40 people would have gone to jail over the scandal and the president would have been forced to resign his office in disgrace. Up until it was resolved, there was a chain of lies, deceptions, half-truths and other nefarious activities that shook Americans' confidence in their democracy to its core.

Art imitates life, of course, and the films that came out after Watergate oftentimes stretched the extent of their plots and the ruthless activities of their antagonists to match the new sensibility about how power corrupts.

Nixon had several targets in his sights. He was vehemently opposed to the anti-war movement that had sprouted up around the Vietnam War and sought to crush it at any opportunity. He started labeling the people who led it as threats and started using intelligence agencies to spy on certain individuals.

Nixon was also notoriously anti-Semitic. Even though some of his most trusted advisors and staffers were Jewish, he regarded Jews as untrustworthy, more concerned with their own community than the nation, and referred to them as "bastards" and by other epithets.

Essentially, Nixon was a paranoid, authoritarian manipulator with no regard for the law or the constitutional limitations on his powers. He saw enemies behind every failure and held to obnoxious racial prejudices.

The conspiracy thinking gets even more fuel due to Nixon's connections with leaders who followed him. According to JTA, a news site for the Jewish community, some of the infamous tapes that Nixon made feature George H.W. Bush and Ronald Regan offering their support while Nixon was going through the Watergate scandal.

There is much more to learn about this scandal and the players involved. The Pentagon Papers, secret expansions of the Vietnam War, wiretapping journalists and more all turned out to be part of Nixon's activities and the massive conspiracies he led to keep them secret.

Some conspiracy theories rest on threadbare evidence, poor understandings of science and government and, in some cases, outright lies. Others, however, are entirely real, including Nixon's illegal activities. It's no wonder that, when we take a look at the paranoid thrillers of the 1970s, we'll see some indications of how much Watergate and the political assassinations in the years surrounding the scandal—John F Kennedy, Bobby

Kennedy, Martin Luther King, Malcolm X and others—brought about a lot of suspicion of government in the population and in the entertainment at the theaters.

Watching it in Film

The paranoid thrillers of the 1970s oftentimes reference, either directly or indirectly, Watergate and political assassinations, sometimes tying a crooked president to the assassinations at some level.

Nixon's paranoia, in some regards, was built around ideas that some people were inherently disloyal to the US—at least as he saw it—and sought to bring it down. Films such as *The Manchurian Candidate* rather play on this type of paranoia.

In the films that came out after Watergate, however, there is oftentimes a theme of intelligence agencies and other shady operators working at the behest of fascistic and murderous officials. The officials are not always revealed, but the conspiracy is.

Looking at some of the 1970s paranoid thrillers in this book it is easy enough to see.

In *Marathon Man*, the exact workings and purpose of The Division, for which the protagonist's brother and one of the main antagonists work, is unclear. All that is clear about it is that the organization murders people and that it has dealt with former Nazis. Given that there was so much frothing at the mouth anti-Semitism in the White House that was exposed due to the Watergate scandal, it's not hard to believe that some government officials would be able to overlook or, in fact, even sympathize with the activities of some of these war criminals.

At the time—and even today—those war criminals were still

out there and World War 2 was only 30 years in the past. Some of the suspicions that were widely held of government officials are best summed up in the term crypto-fascist. This is an individual who has fascist sympathies or who may, in fact, outright consider themselves to be a fascist, but who keeps those beliefs close to the vest and doesn't discuss them openly.

When high-ranking officials are having anti-Semitic conversations behind closed doors, using intelligence agencies to monitor political opponents secretly, seeking to damage the reputations of those political opponents and believing that they should be able to operate without accountability, it's easy to see how someone might suspect that there are crypto-fascists at work.

Combine this with the fact that many people suspected that JFK was assassinated by a conspiracy and that some of the information in the Warren Commission report seems counterintuitive and you have a perfect recipe for the other paranoia that frequently pops up in the thrillers of the 1970s.

The paranoia is based on the idea that there are powerful forces in the government that actively seek to suppress information about the crimes they commit. Traitors and interlopers are not tolerated. Essentially, any government crime gets investigated by a panel that is all too willing to leave important questions unanswered and even unasked. The commission will also bend its findings to accommodate the most powerful political figures, ensuring that they remain safe from ever being held accountable for their crimes.

The Parallax View is one of the finest examples of this type of paranoia being worked into a conspiracy thriller. *Capricorn One* also shows a complex collusion of high-ranking officials who want to cover up a murderous and wide-ranging conspiracy and who have control of enough federal power to make sure it happens.

The Theme to Watch For

The theme of many of the paranoid thrillers from the 1970s is that the biggest threat to freedom and fairness comes from within the US government. These thrillers reflect a distrust of government that became socially very significant at the time. There is a tradition of distrust in government in the US, but there's an interesting way that conspiracy theories and films about them have evolved since Watergate.

Consider the Business Plot. There is debate as to how far this really went, but the basics of the story are that a group of businessmen approached former general Smedley Butler in the 1930s about a plot to overthrow the US government. They'd use an army of veterans to intimidate Roosevelt into having to integrate a new secretarial position into the government, a position that would give the person who held it dictatorial powers. Smedley was approached to fill that role, but exposed the plot. It's considered to be credible by many historians, but it's not clear how far it really got.

What's important is that this conspiracy theory represents a threat from *outside* the government; a threat to freedom, democracy and the US system of government in general. Nixon was a real-life example of a threat to those same things from *within* the government. He was worse than the Business Plot in ways, since he really did ascend to take control of the levers of power.

In 1970s paranoid thrillers, look for plots that focus on threats from within. They may be corrupt politicians, intelligence agencies or even science agencies, but they will already be in power and will mean to hold on to it. These aren't clandestine actions taken against the US government that are at issue in these films. There's no communist sleeper agent, as in *The Manchurian Candidate*. These are films where the real threat is from people who are in charge of the government and its powers, but who don't believe in freedom or democracy.

Quite often, a conglomeration of interests within the military-industrial complex are the real culprits and officials all the way up to the president might be little more than puppets. It's as if the Business Plot had won, but there was no visible coup to alert the people that something had changed, and horribly.

A Specific Representation

In *The Parallax View*, among the first representatives of the power that the protagonist encounters are a sheriff and his deputy. The protagonist is a rebel, has long hair for the era and dresses very casually, even sloppily. The deputy questions his masculinity, calls him female outright as a sort of misogynistic insult and initiates a fistfight. The protagonist is the outsider, representing freedom, curiosity, new ways of thinking and a sense of justice. He threatens American institutions of power, and that's why we trust him. The representative of the system is no heroic deputy. He's a bigoted, violent, bullying fascist type who has the blessings of his superior to tear apart a bar attacking a man for the crime of having long hair and seeming a bit outside the mainstream. The insiders are corrupt and only outsiders should be trusted.

It's quite a reversal from the pre-Watergate era, where many of the threats came from outside the system and the protagonist was trying to preserve American government rather than trying to save the US from it.

Corporate Conspiracies Become Important

Corporations are increasingly becoming a part of modern paranoia thrillers, and for good reason. There have been many instances of corporations covering up information that could be damaging to them and their profits. Put this sort of activity in a nation where there is little or no law to protect those who would serve as whistleblowers and things can get very intense very quickly.

The Constant Gardener is a good example of films that use corporate conspiracies to provide the tension and the paranoia. In that film, the antagonist is a drug company, testing drugs on a population that has no idea they're being given something very dangerous. The reason is quite simply that, were the drug company to test these drugs in the US or a nation where there was more regulation, they couldn't get it approved fast enough to get it on the market before competitors brought something else on the market. The dangerous drug plotline was based in a specific case involving the company Pfizer.

Pfizer has been implicated in testing in Africa that took the lives of several children. A documentary about the case was released by the BBC. The story in *The Constant Gardener* is fictionalized, but in making a disclaimer stating as much, the author of the novel on which the film is based, John Le Carre, said that his novel is tame compared to what he learned about the practices of such companies.

The point is that, like the films of the 1970s that mirrored what happened with the Watergate scandal, many of the paranoid thrillers of today actually have much to do with real life events. The film *Silkwood* tells the story of a nuclear power worker who became a whistleblower and who died under suspicious circumstances.

There are always those who find a great deal of paranoia in the plots of these films and, of course, that's part of the point.

However, many of them have a basis in reality. Corporations sometimes have billions of dollars riding on a product, such as a pharmaceutical, and it's conceivable that, somewhere in that immense corporate structure, there would be those who are willing to go too far to protect their profits and their company.

Other films play on this theme with different industries. *Syriana*, for instance, involves oil companies. Whatever the company might be making, if there is sufficient profit involved, there is always room for a conspiracy. Make that company part of the military-industrial complex and you have even more cause to be a bit paranoid.

The ultimate film that covers corporate conspiracies, however, may be *The Insider* and, if that's what you want to see on the screen, be sure to put that one high on your list of must-watch films.

Part 2: The Films

The following section contains major spoilers. If you haven't seen these films and don't want to know what goes on in the plots before you do, watch the film first. The plot section will usually serve to clear up some things that might not have come across on screen easily, which is common in these films, given their complexity.

The films featured in this section contain some of the best films out of the paranoid thriller genre and, beyond that, they also include some that aren't quite as well known as the huge names out there. Everyone's heard of *All the President's Men* and *Silkwood*, but not as many have likely heard of or seen *The Parallax View* or *Capricorn One*.

The breakdowns of the films that follow concentrate on the plot and story rather than the technical elements of the films. They should provide you with a route to find more films along the lines of the ones you end up liking a great deal.

Again, spoilers ahead!

The Man Who Knew Too Much (1956)

Director:

Alfred Hitchcock

Starring:

James Stewart

Doris Day

The Man Who Knew Too Much was made into a film twice by Hitchcock, once in 1934 and once in 1956. This section covers the latter of those films, starring James Stewart and Doris Day. The title sums up the plot well; the film follows a man who gets information on a major assassination about to take place in England while he's on vacation in Morocco.

The Plot

The film opens up with a line about cymbal crashes changing someone's life. The action then goes to Morocco, where Dr. Ben McKenna, his wife Josephine and their son Hank are all on vacation. While they're on the bus, Hank accidently pulls a woman's veil off. The husband, offended, berates the young boy. A Frenchman named Bernard intervenes, calming the man down and explaining that the man was just mad because the women in the country don't take their veils off in public.

Bernard is friendly, but Jo notices that he gets a lot of personal information out of Ben, but that he tells Ben virtually nothing about himself. Bernard wants to take the couple out for a dinner.

Jo presses the issue and begins to ask Bernard more specific questions about himself in their hotel room. He evades them all. While they're all getting ready to go out for a drink, a man comes to the door and suspiciously says that he was looking for another room. Bernard soon cancels the dinner plans.

Jo and Ben go to dinner and run into another couple, Edward and Lucy. Bernard shows up but doesn't acknowledge Jo and Ben, deeply offending Ben.

The next day, while exploring Marrakesh with Edward and Lucy, Bernard runs up to Ben, a knife sticking out of his back. Ben realizes that Bernard has his face painted brown to make his skin look darker and is wearing Arab clothing. He drops dead, but not before whispering something in Ben's ear. In London, there is an assassination plot against a foreign statesman. He gives Ben the name Ambrose Chappell and tells him to notify the authorities.

Ben and Jo go to the police station to make a statement, leaving Hank with Edward and Lucy. They find out that Bernard was actually a French intelligence service agent. Ben then gets a call. It warns him that Hank has been kidnapped and that he is not to repeat whatever Bernard told him to anyone.

The couple heads to London. There they meet Inspector Buchanan of Scotland Yard. He knows what Bernard was working on and tells Ben and Jo to call him if the kidnappers make contact.

Ben finds a man named Ambrose Chappell in the phone book and sets up a meeting. He goes to the man's store—he's a taxidermist—but the man knows nothing of assassination plots.

Ben barely makes it out of the taxidermist shop without being arrested.

Jo figures out that it might not be a name but a place. She finds a church named Ambrose Chappell and she and Ben rendezvous there. They attend part of a service. Jo sneaks out to call the police and Ben keeps an eye on Edward and Lucy, who are posing as the priest and a worker at the chapel. Ben gets hit over the head and locked in the chapel. The kidnappers take Hank to a foreign embassy, where there is little the police can do.

Ben makes it out of the chapel and Jo finds out that Buchanan is at the Royal Albert Hall. She goes to find the inspector to get his help.

The assassin, the same man who came to the hotel door in Marrakesh and said he was at the wrong room, tells Jo that Hank's fate depends upon her actions. A foreign prime minister has come to see the show and Jo figures out that he's the target.

The assassin is waiting for a moment in the music when the cymbals crash loudly, which will cover the sound of his handgun. Jo sees the assassin and Ben tries to get to him. As the assassin brings his weapon up to aim at the prime minister, Jo screams, startling him and running his aim. He wings the prime minister.

Ben gets to the assassin and fights with him, with the assassin falling off the balcony to his death. The prime minister insists that Ben and Jo come to his embassy so he can thank them for saving his life.

They go to the embassy and Jo, an accomplished singer, agrees to sing for the group. She starts singing "Que Sera, Sera", which she sings with Hank at the beginning of the film. They suspect that Hank is at the embassy and, when Hank whistles in response to the song, they find him.

The plot turns out to have been hatched by the ambassador from the same nation as the prime minister. Ben fights with one of the conspirators, knocking him down the stairs and killing him when his own gun goes off.

The film ends as Ben and Jo come back to their London hotel and reunite with some of Jo's friends, who had been waiting for them through the entire London ordeal.

Hitchcock Moments

There are some great moments in this film that any Hitchcock fan who hasn't seen it will very much appreciate. In particular, when Ben is walking down a London street, a second sound of footfalls other than his own becomes particularly sinister, to the point where it's nearly unbearable.

Hitchcock liked putting regular people in extraordinary situations, and this film does just that. Ben and Jo are not equipped to deal with the type of situation they find themselves in. Jo is clearly the brighter of the two, recognizing right away that the suspicious people around them in Marrakesh were, in fact, suspicious. Ben seemed more or less oblivious the entire time.

Both characters, however, come through when it counts. Ben manages to fight off some dangerous people—it's revealed that he's a World War 2 vet, so this is believable—and Jo has a very good head on her shoulders. Like Stewart's love interest in *Rear Window*, she provides him with a tremendous advantage in her perceptiveness and intelligence and, when it comes to it, courage.

There is really no reason to not watch any Hitchcock film. He's one of the best. This film is a great thriller, not as dark as some of his other films, but still very effective. Where it fits in as a paranoid thriller among the others in this book, however, is also interesting.

The Outside Threat

This film deals with an outside threat to a government, and a government that's not even the protagonist's own. The prime minister and the ambassador that want him dead are not part of the US government, which makes this film quite a bit different than the post-Watergate thrillers that are really some of the best of this genre.

There's no conspiracy here to fool an entire society into believing something false, to take over a government through clandestine activities or anything else along those lines. This film's plot centers on a relatively straightforward assassination attempt and a man who gets way closer to it than he wants to.

The investigation arc in this film is different than in the later films you'll see. In this film, the investigation doesn't really peel back layers and layers of conspiracy. It simply involves finding out who Ambrose is and getting word to him, and finding Hank. It's a straightforward plot in this regard.

The Man Who Knew Too Much will come off much differently than many of the other films featured in this book, and not simply because it was directed by Hitchcock and, therefore, has his style and benefits from his excellent filmmaking. This film has a completely different type of plot than most of the other films in this book and is worth watching. The opening assassination is a great example of this, as it happens in a foreign land where Ben doesn't even know the applicable table manners. It's got nothing to do with domestic political intrigue and, in fact, Ben and Jo are fishes out of water in just about every regard in this film, including dealing with foreign conspiracy plots.

Enjoying this Paranoid Thriller

The Man Who Knew Too Much is a beautiful film to look at. Every aspect of the filmmaking is well done here and there are some scenes that are really standouts. The use of sound in this film, particularly in the aforementioned street scene, is also great. The entire plot, in fact, centers on a particular sound, which will conceal the gunshot. It's hard to believe that this would work in real life—guns are really loud, of course—but it fits in with the entire theme of the film.

Jo is an accomplished singer and, being played by Doris Day, they found excuses to have her sing in this film. She does have a great voice and her theater friends who show up near the end of the film are a fun bunch. Between those two things, she comes off as a credible theater star or, at least, one who was one at one time. She's not a scared and screaming female love interest and Day plays Jo as very sharp, smart and brave.

Stewart is also great in this film, showing his ability to come off as an irritable, usually irritated man who is also likeable for some reason, nonetheless. He doesn't suddenly become a great fighter or show a natural ability to navigate the dangerous world that Bernard's last words thrust him into and, in fact, he bumbles his efforts a lot. This makes the character very relatable, however. He's a doctor from Indianapolis whose son got kidnapped because a spy told him information he probably wouldn't have cared about anyway. It's a great motivation to put someone utterly unprepared in a dangerous situation, and Stewart does a good job here.

This film is not as intense as modern paranoid thrillers usually are. It's downright lighthearted at times and, particularly for Hitchcock's work, it has a much less serious tone than one might expect. It still works, however, and there are some scenes here where the characters are clearly in real danger.

This film was shot in VistaVision, which gives it a very wide aspect ratio. If you happen to watch it on a projector or on a large television screen, the camerawork really stands out for being as good as it is. Hitchcock clearly put a great deal of thought into what appeared in every frame and it's worth getting the DVD release of this film, which was released in 2000.

If you're a fan of Hitchcock, you'll certainly enjoy this film and likely have seen it already. If you're just exploring this director or paranoid thrillers in general, this is a great film for getting an idea of what they were like before Watergate and before the plots and conspiracies started mirroring the events of that scandal.

The Parallax View (1974)

Director:

Alan J. Pakula

Starring:

Hume Cronyn

Paula Prentiss

Warren Beatty

William Daniels

The Parallax View is a tense, dark thriller that plays on Watergate-era conspiracy theories and JFK and RFK assassination conspiracies. It doesn't hit them directly, but it certainly hits all the right notes in showing a very sinister, powerful conspiracy and how a reporter uncovers it.

The Plot
The film opens up at a political rally in Seattle. Charles Carroll, a senator who's running for president, is assassinated in the Space Needle. One of the assassins is thrown off the top of the monument by bodyguards, while the other escapes.

A congressional committee concludes that there was only one gunman responsible for the assassination. Reporter Lee Carter, however, witnessed the assassination and she is in fear for her life. She used to date the protagonist, Joe Frady, and she seeks him out for help.

The people who witnessed the Carroll assassination have been dying off and Lee believes that she's going to be killed. Frady dismisses her concerns, but she turns up dead, apparently the result of an overdose.

Frady ends up going to a small town to investigate the deaths. He almost immediately gets into a bar fight with a local deputy, which the local sheriff, who is sitting nearby, allows to go on, breaking up the bar. Frady eventually talks to the sheriff and the sheriff gives Frady some information on one of the murders.

Later, Frady is checking out the scene of the suspected murder when the sheriff shows up to kill him. Frady fights him off, killing him in a torrent of water unleashed by an opening dam.

Frady steals the sheriff's car and leads the deputies on a pursuit. After crashing into a supermarket, he gets away. When he goes back to his offices, he finds out that the Sheriff's Department doesn't want to press charges, which Frady sees as further proof of wanting to cover something up.

Frady, while rifling through the sheriff's possessions, finds a questionnaire from the Parallax Corporation, a psychological exam for new hires. Frady has an expert take a look at the questionnaire and figure out what kind of answers a true killer would give.

Frady tracks down another one of the witnesses to Carroll's assassination. The man meets him on a boat and gives him more information about the plot surrounding the assassination. The boat blows up, however, and Frady is assumed to be dead.

Frady shows up at his editor's office and gives his editor the information that he has thus far. He then poses as someone else and applies to the Parallax Corporation. He is accepted and brought into the corporation for further training.

He is made to watch a film that shows various images, some horrific and some pleasant. He sits through the apparent brainwashing, or testing, and is apparently hired on fully.

Frady sees the assassin who escaped after Carroll's murder at the Parallax Corporation. He tails him, seeing him apparently make a pickup and a delivery to the airport. Frady tries to follow the package and finds a senator on the plane. He writes a warning that there is a bomb on the plane, forcing it to land. It blows up soon after getting back on the ground.

Frady has been sending information back to his editor, and he sends a conversation that reveals the nature of Parallax. The editor is poisoned, however, by an assassin from Parallax who tampers with his delivery food.

Frady goes to a political rally rehearsal for another senator, on the trail of the Parallax assassins. He hides and watches. The Parallax assassins shoot the senator while he's driving across the arena on a golf cart. Frady realizes that he's their patsy and tries to get away.

He nearly makes it out of the arena, but is met at the door by another Parallax assassin, who shoots him dead.

The ending mirrors the beginning of the film, with a senate committee finding that Hammond's assassin acted alone and that he was mentally ill. They admonish those who would launch conspiracy theories over the assassination and close the hearings.

JFK Conspiracy Allegory

It's hard to imagine that one person can change the world. It might be a widely held romantic notion, but most thinking people realize that one person seldom does. Perhaps that's the problem when a major political assassination is investigated and all signs point to a single person, not particularly well trained or connected, changing the course of history in one horrible act. It's hard to believe, and that's what *The Parallax View* uses to keep the plot going.

The entire plot mirrors what most JFK assassination conspiracy theories hold to be true in various ways. Behind at least some political assassinations carried out by one person is actually a network of powerful, unaccountable people who actually do the killing. The person named as the killer is a patsy of some sort.

The Parallax Corporation takes all the various players usually named as the organization behind the JFK assassination—the mafia, anti-communist groups, the intelligence agencies, etc.— and puts in their place a corporation. This is not a corporation that kills as a way to protect their business interests; the Parallax Corporation's profits come directly from killing, as much as we see.

There is collusion with the government, however. The senate panel shown at the end of the film—which is obviously a stand-in for the Warren Commission—has to be going along with the Parallax Corporation. It would seem that any FBI agent worth their paycheck would be able to start connecting the dots between the various murders and figure out that they're all connected. The film gives the impression that there are some things the government never means to have discovered and that it may be behind some political assassinations. The assassinated politicians in this film are described as outsiders and mavericks, implying that they're some sort of threat to the existing order.

The Parallax View doesn't really try to say that any particular assassination was carried out by a specific conspiracy. It's not a film that purports to tell any particular truth but, instead, is a very effective thriller built on a foundation laid by many different conspiracy theories that have one thing in common. All of those conspiracy theories involve an assassination that was carried out by a single shooter, but hold that the single shooter theory is a ruse and that there was a powerful organization—or several organizations working together—behind the murder.

Enjoying this Paranoid Thriller

The Parallax View is a pure paranoid thriller. It doesn't try to tell the audience that it's delivering the truth behind any assassination, but it plays on theories surrounding several of them. We have a corporation that exists only to murder and a series of political assassinations that are pinned on a lone gunman. Of course, this will sound familiar to anyone who knows their 1960s theory, or their conspiracy theories.

The film moves along briskly. The protagonist is likeable enough to be interesting and flawed enough to be fun. He's not a particularly nice or reliable person, but he's fearless and curious and doesn't give up once he gets the idea that he's on to something.

Like many films of this nature, there are killings that are set up so that they may or may not have been assassinations. There are inconsistencies in them that make them curious enough to merit further investigation. The dam that was supposed to have opened up and drowned one witness, for instance, was equipped with an incredibly loud and audible siren, making it unlikely that the victim would have unknowingly been washed away.

There are some excellent tense scenes in this film. Several of the most intense scenes, including the fight at the top of the Space Needle, don't have music behind them, which makes them markedly different from most such scenes today. The sound effects are subdued and watching it seems almost like watching an amateur or documentary film of the event, which makes it more visceral.

This film plays on the idea that outsiders that threaten the order of things become tests. It also plays on the idea that, when those targets make themselves a nuisance, the people in power have ways to deal with it and are unaccountable for anything that they do. This should make it appealing to anyone who likes conspiracy thrillers that are based on real life conspiracy theories, but that are not dedicated to shoring them up.

Three Days of the Condor (1975)

Director:

Sydney Pollack

Starring:

Cliff Robertson

Faye Dunaway

Max von Sydow

Robert Redford

Three Days of the Condor is an excellent paranoid thriller set in the Watergate era, when suspicion was running high, and for good reason. This thriller follows a man whose CIA comrades are hit by professionals as he explores an apparent cover-up.

The Plot

Joe Turner is a CIA worker who's so far from being a field operative that he doesn't use his code name enough to know it reflexively. He's a brain. He works with several other intelligence workers sorting through media from around the globe, trying to discern whether messages are being sent or ideas being propagated through them.

Joe has been investigating a book. There's nothing remarkable about it and it seems to be no more than an average mystery/thriller novel. Joe, however, locks on to the fact that it's only been translated into a few languages—Dutch, Arabic and Spanish—which strikes him as strange. He files a report on the matter.

He gets lunch duty one afternoon and goes out to get food for his fellow workers. While he's away, a group of assassins storm the building where he works, which is a front called the American Literary Historical Society, and kills everyone, including a female coworker with whom Joe seems particularly close.

Joe comes back to find his coworkers dead, takes a gun from the desk of the secretary at the front of the building and contacts his superiors. They tell him that they'll need to bring him back in. When Joe turns up for the meeting with the agents that are supposed to get him to safety, however, it's an ambush. He wounds a CIA assassin and one of his other friends at the agency is killed.

Realizing that there's some sort of a conspiracy and that he needs to stay underground, he abducts Kathy Hale, who he sees purchasing clothes for a ski trip. He goes to her apartment, passes out for a while out of exhaustion and then sees the evening news, which describes the scene of the ambush where Joe was nearly killed. It's written off as a murder and the gunman is said to still be at large.

Joe and Kathy get to know one another and eventually sleep together. The next morning, one of the same hitmen who killed off the workers at the American Literary Historical Society shows up at Kathy's apartment and tries to kill Joe. They get into a vicious fight, with Joe eventually killing the man.

Joe figures out that the CIA itself seems to be out to kill him. He keeps talking to his superior, Higgins, but there is a great deal of mistrust. Eventually, Kathy approaches Higgins in a restaurant and she and Joe kidnap him.

Joe interrogates Higgins and finds out that a man named Joubert, a Frenchman, was the man who killed his co-workers and who tried to kill Joe.

Higgins starts to look into the matter himself, realizing that there must be something going on within the CIA. He finds out that the hitman who Joe killed in Kathy's apartment was a former Marine who had started working for the CIA as part of his "detached" service. The man was associated with Joubert.

Joe figures out where to find Joubert. He traces a phone call and gets another name, Atwood, a man that Joubert was talking to on the phone. Joe shows up at Atwood's house, puts on some music to wake him up and then interrogates him at gunpoint. He finds out that the reason that the novel Joe was working on was translated into those specific languages is that those nations are all oil exporting nations. It was concealed information and Joe had inadvertently discovered a plan to start a war in the Middle East over oil.

Joubert shows up and disarms Joe. He walks over to Atwood and shoots him in the head, staging the scene so that it looks like a suicide. Joubert explains that Atwood had hired him to kill Joe and his coworkers, but that the situation has changed and the CIA has hired Joubert to kill Atwood.

With no reason to kill Joe, Joubert is friendly and gives Joe some advice. He explains that Joe should get out of the country, preferably to Europe. He then explains how Joe is likely to be hit, giving him some insight into what to expect.

Joe gets a ride back to New York City. He meets with Higgins and, as Joubert predicted, there's a car slowing down alongside the men. Joe tells Higgins to wave the car on and then walks down the street with him.

Higgins explains that the oil plan is to ensure that, in the event that there is a shortage, people will have oil. He explains that it could be food or anything else, but if the people run out, they won't care how the government obtains the resources that they need, they'll just want the government to come through with them.

Joe reveals that he divulged what he knew to the *New York Times*. Higgins says that it will never get published, but Joe maintains that it will. Joe walks off into the crowd and the film ends.

A Great Paranoia Thriller

Being set near the time when Watergate was exploding and when suspicion of the government was very high, this thriller really cranks up the conspiracy angle. There are conspiracies everywhere. There are conspiracies within the CIA and there are conspiracies that are just the official business of the CIA. No matter where Joe turns, he's a marked man and has no one he can really trust. In fact, the only honest people in this film, really, are Kathy and Joubert. Kathy isn't involved at all and Joubert, surprisingly, is a hitman, but one who only does what he's paid for and has nothing personal against his targets.

There are some great scenes in this film that really speak to the murkiness of intelligence in the modern era. When talking with a much older superior, Higgins asks if the veteran intelligence officer misses the sort of action that he saw in World War 2 and before. The old man says he doesn't miss the action, but that he misses the clarity. It's telling. In those days, there was a clear enemy, at least according to this operative, and there was purpose. In the modern era, everything is double-crosses, double-dealing, double-agents and double everything else.

Joe is a great character. There is some rather primitive computer research in this film and Joe and the other workers at the Literary Society are computerizing what they find out, but the character is really the computer in this movie. Joe has a tremendous ability to take in and process information. He sees connections and has a tremendous capacity to remember facts. The computers of the era were, of course, slow and ponderous affairs, but Joe's mind is fast and sharp.

Where the computers are concerned, there are some great scenes in this film that show them as nearly mystical machines. In one, Higgins is researching the hitmen and the computer shows a video of a car blowing up, as if it just knows that this is important information that the operator needs to see. It's interesting in that the computer is used for exposition and technical flash, but it really doesn't keep up with Joe in any regard. Higgins gets facts and connections out of the data that the CIA has, but Joe seems to be able to lock on to the "why" of the situation. That's what makes him dangerous. He has an incredible ability to recall information and to make connections, but he also has the sort of intense creativity required to get into that information enough to understand why something is happening.

There are some oddities in this film in the way that some of the characters behave. This is, of course, form the 1970s. That influences how the government and intelligence agencies are portrayed, but it also has a very strong influence on how the characters relate to one another.

A Really Sweet Guy

Kathy proves to be resilient, tough and brave. She's also stunning, played by Faye Dunaway, so this isn't a woman who is likely to be suffering from a lack of options in lovers or partners. There are allusions to her being essentially lonely and having a hard time connecting but, nonetheless, it would seem like most anyone would be interested in her.

Joe kidnaps her at gunpoint. He takes her back to his apartment, puts her in a wrestling hold so she can sleep. The then goes on very paranoid rants about what's going on. The viewer knows that what Joe's saying is true, but it would sound like utter nonsense to anyone who didn't know that and, when you add to that the fact that Joe has a gun, it gets even more frightening.

Joe then roughs Kathy up a bit—he doesn't hit her, but certainly overpowers her—ties her up and gags her and leaves her in the bathroom while he steals her car. He comes back that night and she confronts him about the violence and he points out that he hasn't raped her. She points out that the night is still young.

They end up having sex. The next morning, she tells Joe that he seems like a "sweet" guy. One wonders what a man had to do to be a bad guy in the 1970s, given that Joe has already committed several violent crimes against Kathy and she finds him "sweet".

Kathy's a great character for the era, but women most certainly get more dignity in today's films. It would be hard to imagine a modern female character putting up with this sort of abuse and then falling in love—or at least lust—with the protagonist. Fortunately for the film, both Redford and Dunaway have incredible charisma on screen, so it makes it somewhat easier to take, but it's still a bit disturbing in that it implies that Joe basically beats a woman into submission and then she falls for him, and then even risks her life for him.

No matter how lonely her photography may have indicated she was there's something really disturbing in how their relationship plays out.

Enjoying this Paranoid Thriller

Despite its odd relationship dynamics, this is a great film. Redford is excellent in the lead role and he's believable throughout the entire film. He doesn't have handgun training, we're told that when the CIA starts to dig into his files, but it's easy to believe that he's just smart enough to figure it out on his own. He doesn't come off as murderous, but he's no one's victim and that makes Joe a great character. The film does us the service of setting him up so that his investigation into what's going on is believable. Joe isn't driven by some moral crusade or a quest for vengeance. He cannot, however, let go of a puzzle once he sees one. He has to solve it. It's something at the core of his being and he desperately—to the point of risking his life—has to know *why* this is all happening to him. He's a great surrogate for the audience, as we find out how deep this all goes and just how dirty these intelligence agencies really are.

It's also refreshing, particularly in today's era of techno-paranoia, to see CIA spooks and intelligence analysts using their brains to figure out what they need to know. They don't have security cameras on every corner, cell phones, GPS locators, fast and portable computers or anything else to help them. Joubert, in fact, figures out where Joe is going to show up because it's a predicable move. These guys aren't video gamers, they're chess players. They play chess on a personal level with one another, with Joe trying to stay one move ahead of experienced intelligence officers and killers. On the international level, they play chess with the economics of entire nations, using war as their tool to get what they want.

There was a lot going on in the 1970s that plays into this film. Watergate is the most obvious influence and, as is the case in many films of this era, the corruption we see here goes all the way up to the top of the agency and its policies. This was also the era when the Energy Crisis was hitting full steam. The idea that people would be clamoring to be able to fill up their cars and that they really wouldn't care how the government got their oil is entirely believable.

Higgins, at the end, makes a very pragmatic statement about what people like him do. There are limited resources in the world and the US needs them to keep on going. While what he says might be callous and cynical, it's hard to argue with his logic. If the gas were to run out, the food were to run out or other vital resources disappeared, it's hard to believe that chaos wouldn't follow in short order.

Redford is the younger generation here. He needs to know why, to understand and to get to the bottom of all this corruption. In the end, he gives it to the newspaper, but it's not clear whether or not that will help. It might never even get reported, as Higgins implies, and the final look we get at Joe is ambiguous.

This is a must-see film. The acting is top-notch, the story is compelling and pulling the layers back on the conspiracy only makes it more engaging. Anyone who likes a good paranoid thriller should find this outstanding.

Marathon Man (1976)

Director:

John Schlesinger

Starring:

Dustin Hoffman

Laurence Olivier

Marthe Keller

Roy Scheider

William Devane

Marathon Man is an intense thriller that follows a Ph.D. candidate who runs into some of the deadliest imaginable people. This is among the films in this book that are truly standouts, and it is definitely worth seeing by anyone, whether or not paranoid thriller style movies interest them in general.

The Plot

Hoffman plays Babe. Babe is a gifted student, going for his Ph.D. in history, whose father was also an historian. He's on his way to becoming a classic absent-minded, eccentric professor by every indication. His apartment is messy; he's awkward with romance and is obsessive about running. The action takes place in New York, for the most part. Early in the film, we see a road rage incident between two old men. One of them is Jewish and the other German. The German man calls the Jewish man Jude, revealing his accent, and the fight escalates. They both die when they get into a wreck with an oil delivery truck.

Babe has a brother, Doc, who Babe believes to be high up in an oil company. In reality, Doc is a government agent. He works for an agency called "The Division". Doc is dangerous, killing a man who tries to assassinate him in a hotel in hand-to-hand fighting.

Babe meets a Swiss woman named Elsa, who he's very excited about.

The old German man killed in the car wreck at the outset of the film was named Szell. He was the brother of Dr. Christian Szell, a wanted war criminal and former Nazi. Szell is hiding out in South America, but knows that his brother had a fortune in diamonds. Szell wants the diamonds, and Doc knows that Szell will come for them.

Doc goes to New York and meets his brother. They talk about their father, who killed himself after being targeted by McCarthy's investigations when Doc and Babe were children. They go out for dinner with Elsa. Doc presses Elsa with questions about where she grew up and claims to know people she may know. He catches her lying. Worried for Babe, Doc warns him that Elsa is just trying to get citizenship and that she's a fraud. Babe is enraged. The fact that he is suddenly dating a European woman is suspicious is not lost on Doc.

Doc goes to meet with Szell. Szell asks him if he is to be trusted and Doc answers, "No." Doc is angry with Szell for involving his brother and the two argue. Szell has an automatic knife strapped to his wrist and uses it to stab Doc. Doc, mortally wounded, makes it all the way back to Babe's apartment.

After the police show up, another member of The Division, Janeway, gets involved. He tells Babe that Doc was really an agent. Janeway believes that Doc must have told Babe something. Why else would he have made his way to the apartment after being viciously stabbed?

Babe's apartment is broken into while he is in the bathtub. He tries to hide in the bathroom and then call for help, but is abducted and taken to a barren, cinderblock room somewhere in the city. Dr. Szell shows up, having shaved his trademark white hair to appear balding. He asks Babe, "Is it safe?" over and over. Babe has no idea what he wants to hear and answers the question in whatever ways he can think of.

Szell uses a dental pick to torture Babe, driving it into a cavity. He then gives him clove oil. After Szell is done torturing Babe, he's sent back to a room. Janeway shows up, stabs the guard with Babe and kills the other on his way out. He and Babe speed away. Janeway starts pressing Babe for information as they drive. He tells Babe about Szell's plan. Szell is after diamonds that he stole from prisoners at Auschwitz. Janeway is convinced that Babe's brother must have told Babe something before he died. Babe doesn't know anything, however, and Janeway drives him back to Szell.

Szell tortures Babe more, using a drill to bore holes in healthy teeth. After enough of it, Szell is convinced that Babe would have said something if he knew anything and tells his men to get rid of him. Babe manages to get away from Szell's men, who can't keep up with him once he gets a chance to make a run for it.

Babe gets the local street gang to rob his apartment for him, which is being watched. The gang takes some of Babe's possessions, but also brings him new clothes and the gun Babe's father used to kill himself, which Babe held on to.

Babe gets in touch with Elsa and has her meet him. They leave the city and Elsa drives Babe to a farmhouse. He realizes that Elsa is working with Szell and confronts her. Szell's heavies and Janeway show up. They go into the house to talk, but one of Szell's men goes for a gun. Babe shoots him, setting off a firefight in which Janeway guns down the other thug.

Janeway tries to make a trade with Babe: Szell for Doc. Janeway kills Elsa and Babe kills Janeway.

Meanwhile, Szell needs to get an appraisal for his diamond collection, which he's withdrawn from a safe deposit box. He starts going to jewelers in the Diamond District, and is soon recognized by an old man who has a concentration camp tattoo. He makes up a story to cover himself and leaves the shop, but a female holocaust survivor recognizes him on the street and starts shouting his name.

Szell tries to slip into the crowd, but the man from the jewelry shop comes after him. The old woman gets hit while crossing the road and Szell slashes the old man's throat and tries to get away.

Babe is waiting for him and he pulls a gun on him. He takes Szell to a water plant in Central Park. Szell does not believe that Babe will shoot him, but Babe tells him that he may keep as many diamonds as he can swallow. To make Szell start eating them, Babe starts throwing handfuls of diamonds at him, most of them falling into the water below.

Babe and Szell end up getting into a fight after Babe loses his gun. Szell still has the automatic knife up his sleeve and tries to get Babe with it, who evades him. Babe throws the diamonds down a flight of stairs, almost into the water. Szell goes after them and falls on his own knife, killing himself.

Babe tosses his gun into the reservoir outside the water plant and the film ends.

Nazi Hunters

It's implied in this film that Janeway—and whatever The Division is—has worked with and against Szell. He's apparently provided information on other wanted Nazi war criminals when needed, but he's clearly still involved in crime himself, which Janeway is also involved in. It makes the character very shady and so is whatever agency he works for.

Szell embodies the classic image of the Nazi war criminal who evaded justice. He lives in South America and, by the looks of it, he lives quite well. He's got plenty of assets stashed here and there, with the ones he's after in this film being directly taken from the people he victimized while he worked at Auschwitz.

Like Mengele in *The Boys from Brazil*, Szell is both a heartless, psychopathic genius and sadist. He uses his medical background to torture people. The scenes where he uses the dental implements are particularly grueling and, though these scenes are not nearly as graphic as most modern torture scenes, they're still stomach turning at times.

The characters in this film, aside from those who are truly evil, are rather ambiguous all round. Babe is a creep, as his neighbors say, but he's honest about who he is. Everyone around him in this film is some sort of successful and powerful liar, save for Else, who is just a bottom rung thug.

Babe's arc sees him go from terrified to angry to vengeful. Like his father, he's being pursued by greedy, power-hungry and sadistic men. Babe's father lost his life—through suicide—to McCarthyism. Babe, on the other hand, uses his father's suicide gun to kill his own tormentors.

This film has many layers to it and can be seen in many different ways. Everything in the film, however, is sinister. The score is sinister. The hostile cityscape of New York in the 1970s is sinister. Szell is beyond sinister, and so is Janeway. There is no comfort for Babe in this film, only increasing levels of pain and fear. Despite its darkness, however, this film is essentially optimistic. In the end, Babe steps up, proves as tenacious and tough as his brother and takes apart a conspiracy of truly evil men.

Enjoying this Paranoid Thriller
Marathon Man is a high-class film. It has great actors giving excellent performances. It's slower than most modern thrillers and spends a lot of time setting up the characters. What keeps it interesting, however, is that the viewer is always aware that those characters are headed somewhere very dark. The music says it, the shooting style says it and the increasingly dangerous people that become part of the story say it. The film delivers on what it sets up.

The film never gets so deep into the conspiracy that it detracts from the story. In this movie, the conspiracy really isn't the heart of the story. The characters are. The conspiracy happens between Janeway, Szell, Elsa and the others, but the viewer is kept an outsider to it. It's impossible to tell what's true and what's not, and no one can be trusted.

Szell is one of the most frightening villains in any film. He's cold, sadistic and determined. He can change his demeanor as best suits him, seeming to have no attachment at all to what he's actually feeling or the people around him. It's all just a front to cover up how incredibly evil this person is.

This film was made in the era where the Nazi war criminals who had escaped were very old and when many of them had likely died off already. The holocaust survivors in the Diamond District are also very old, but the film emphasizes how sadistic Szell was by showing how quickly these characters recognize him. Decades after the war ended and long enough to change what a person looks like, these elderly people instantly recognized Szell's face. The world around them, however, has already forgotten, not knowing the name Szell at all, apparently, or the nickname the prisoners had given him.

Babe encounters evil from before he was born; his father is taken away from him by the evil and paranoia of his childhood and now he encounters men like Janeway—the latest generation of powerful, unaccountable and endlessly corrupt men. In this film, however, unlike many others in this genre, the right people pull through in the end. It works out well for babe, but underneath it all there's the sense of multi-generational corruption and secrecy and that, much of the time, the bad guys win and are never held accountable.

Capricorn One (1977)

Director:

Peter Hyams

Starring:

Brenda Vaccaro

David Doyle

David Huddleston

Elliott Gould

Hal Holbrook

James Brolin

James Karen

Karen Black

O. J. Simpson

Sam Waterston

Telly Savalas

Capricorn One builds a vast and deadly conspiracy theory around the first manned mission to Mars. It takes the moon landing conspiracy and turns it into an engaging thriller.

The Plot

The film opens up as the first manned mission to Mars is about to take off. The vice president and his wife are in attendance. Everything seems to be going fine; the astronauts get a warm send off and take their positions in the launch vehicle. Just as the rocket is preparing to blast off, however, Charles Brubaker, John Walker and Peter Willis, the crewmembers, are hurried out of the rocket and flown to a military base.

The rocket launch proceeds, giving the crowd the impression that the crew are on their way. The crew, however, ends up in a plain looking room until Dr. Kelloway, a high-ranking NASA official, comes in to explain what's going on.

The contractor who built the life support system cut corners. NASA became aware that the life support system was going to fail and that the astronauts were doomed. Therefore, they couldn't send them on the mission.

However, NASA and the space program are under intense pressure to perform. The failure of the mission, according to Kelloway, would ruin people's faith in the space program and wind up wiping it out.

The astronauts are told that NASA intends to fake the entire mission. Phony information is being sent back to the control room. At the military base where the astronauts are being held captive, a huge studio set has been constructed. The footage, combined with special effects, will allow the agency to fake footage from the red planet.

The astronauts don't want to go along with the plan, but Kelloway tells them that, if they don't, their families will be killed. With no other real option, the astronauts agree to go along with the hoax.

One of the NASA control center personnel gets strange data from the mission. He analyzes it using his own program and finds it suspicious. He's admonished for using his own program by Kelloway. Later, the NASA worker is having a drink with his friend, Caulfield, at a bar. He brings up the suspicious data. Caulfield goes to take a phone call at the bar. When he returns to the pool table, his friend is gone.

Caulfield tries to track his fried down, but finds a strange woman living in his friend's apartment with rental receipts going back a year. There's no evidence that his friend even existed. Later, Caulfield's car is sabotaged, nearly killing him. After he voices his concerns to his editor and starts poking around more, he's arrested on possession of cocaine, based on evidence that is planted by federal agents.

The crew of the Capricorn One mission completes their hoax. The plan is to fly them to a location outside the predicted landing site, place them in the capsule and have them picked up as if they'd just gotten back from Mars. The return vehicle, however, has a heat shield failure when it enters the atmosphere. The astronauts are flown back to the military base.

The astronauts realize that the conspirators have to kill them. If they showed up alive, the entire conspiracy would be exposed. They steal a plane and fly off into the desert, but find out that the plane has hardly any fuel in it. They crash in the desert and set off in different directions to prevent them from all being captured.

They're hunted down by military helicopters. Charles alone survives.

Caulfield figures out which military base the astronauts were kept at. He shows up and finds it empty. He finds evidence that the astronauts where there, however, and hires a private pilot, who dusts crops for a living, to take him out to search the desert.

They find Charles at an abandoned gas station in the desert. Charles manages to hop on the wing of the plane and get away, with the helicopters in pursuit. Caulfield and Charles escape the pursuers.

The end of the film shows a memorial service for the astronauts, with the media in attendance. Caulfield pulls up with Charles and the news cameras spin around to document the event. The film ends with the two of them walking toward the funeral party, Charlie's family stunned to see him alive.

Making the Moon Hoax Scary

Compared to some of the other conspiracy theories out there, the hoaxing of the moon landing is generally one of the less frightening ones. It mostly centers on analyzing photos and films of the astronauts on the moon and coming up with theories as to why their spacecraft couldn't have made it to the moon.

In this film, however, the conspiracy becomes downright frightening. From the start, it's easy to see that the conspirators would stand to gain a lot—and their conspiracy would be well protected—if they faked the death of the astronauts on reentry. It turns out to be an accident that it becomes necessary, but it's also really the most logical way to keep the conspiracy hidden. After all, two people can keep a secret if one of them is dead, as the saying goes. An entire crew of astronauts—a group of people who aren't known to be scared of much—being scared into silence for the rest of their lives is really a pretty unrealistic scenario.

This puts enough tension into the film to keep it going and, in fact, to keep two separate stories related to the same conspiracy going.

Caulfield provides our curious protagonist for the story. He's an obnoxious, cocky reporter but he's also tenacious about figuring out what happened to his friend. As he digs deeper, things start getting weirder and more frightening and he's hooked.

This film was made in the 70s, of course, so the chases and hit attempts are rather subdued compared to what one might expect in a modern thriller. There aren't a lot of bullets exchanged until the very end of the film, and even then it's still just Caulfield and the crew running for their lives. There's never the sense that they're capable of fighting back, and that makes the film a bit more engaging.

The flight of the astronauts through the desert is some of the tensest material in this film. They suffer mightily and are on the run from military personnel with helicopters. Kelloway knows them well enough to predict their movements, and that makes the situation more perilous still.

When this film does bring together all the players in its sizeable story, the climax is worth it. This film doesn't really break any new ground where conspiracy thrillers and paranoid thrillers are concerned, but it does right by the genre and certainly has some intense moments.

Enjoying this Paranoid Thriller
Capricorn One offers a different plotline than most of the films in this book, based on a less-used conspiracy. The elements that go into most any paranoid thriller are all there, however. We

have the protagonist trying to figure out the conspiracy and another set of protagonists in the astronauts, who are trying to escape it. We have the shady government agency and the information that they don't want to get out to the public. Assassination attempts, ruining people's reputations and outright murder are all employed by the conspirators as tools to keep everything under control, making them appropriately evil.

The acting in the film is good, the characters are interesting and the action sequences are very well done as well. The scenes shot in the desert are really quite effective, and the sense that the astronauts have nowhere to run makes it a very grim story. The viewer knows at least some of these guys are going to get killed, and they did nothing to bring that on themselves.

Caulfield's investigation is done well and the way he exposes the conspiracy is believable. It reaches out to him rather quickly, however, so there's not necessarily that much work for him to do. This film does see him admitting several times that what he's thinking is crazy and that no one would believe him. This makes the character a bit more believable, as no one smart enough to uncover such a conspiracy would believe it even existed without a lot of proof.

Capricorn One is well worth the time investment. It's intense, has great action sequences and a great conspiracy story to hold it all together.

The Boys from Brazil (1978)

Director:

Franklin J. Schaffner

Starring:

Gregory Peck

James Mason

Laurence Olivier

The Boys from Brazil follows a famous Nazi hunter as he searches for Josef Mengele and discovers that the former Auschwitz doctor has launched a terrible plan. Spanning contents, his search leads him closer and closer to one of the most infamous war criminals in history.

The Plot
The film starts out in Paraguay. Kohler is engaging in some amateur Nazi hunting and, through his efforts, discovers where some of the most wanted criminals of the Third Reich have been meeting. He gets photographs of some of the war criminals and tries to persuade Ezra Lieberman, a famous Nazi hunter, to take an interest in the case. Ezra, however, already knows that there are many Third Reich criminals living in Paraguay and doesn't get involved.

Kohler bribes a young boy who watches the gate at a mansion where the Nazis meet. He gives the boy a radio. In return, the boy plants a bug in the living room of the mansion. Kohler sneaks onto the grounds at night and records a meeting.

At the meeting, Kohler hears Josef Mengele greeting several different officers. Mengele then launches into their orders. They'll need to kill 94 different men near specific dates. These men are scattered across several different nations.

While he's listening to the meeting, however, Kohler's friend, the young boy, is tuning into stations on the radio that Kohler gave him. The boy happens across the same frequency the bug is transmitting on and a security guard overhears it. He rushes into the room, sending the Nazis into a frenzy as they search out the bug.

Kohler races back to his hotel room. He calls Ezra and plays a portion of the tape, but Mengele and his thugs have already found the hotel, having interrogated the staff. The Nazis stab Kohler to death and, for a few tense seconds, Mengele and Ezra are on the phone together, though Mengele says nothing. Mengele orders his men to kill the boy.

Ezra thinks that Kohler may have been on to something and decides to follow up on his material. He looks into the deaths of civil servants, which all of the targets seem to be. As he investigates, he finds out that all of the families of the murdered men include an adopted child who looks exactly the same. The child, under various names and in various locations, has jet black hair, pale skin and deep blue eyes. He's also surly, spoiled and rude. Each of the women is around 20 years younger than her deceased husband.

Realizing that there is some sort of a connection, Ezra goes to prison to interview a Nazi war criminal that he hunted down, Frieda Maloney. She worked for the same adoption agency that adopted out the boys to the families.

Ezra then meets with a scientist who works in genetics. The scientist explains how a rabbit was cloned by having its DNA injected into an egg that was drained of its own. The experiment, done on rabbits, resulted in several clones of the same rabbit.

A flashback shows Mengele working in Brazil. In a hospital ward, he has a group of young women, all blond and blue-eyed, whom he is treating. Mengele was using genetic information taken from Hitler himself and using the women to carry the fetus. The resulting Hitler clone was then adopted out to a family that exactly mirrored Hitler's own, his father a civil servant who dies in his 60s—or is killed, in Mengele's plan—his mother doting on him and spoiling him. Mengele has created the clones and, following that, recreated the conditions of Hitler's youth.

Mengele, of course, is not working alone, and the organization of ex-Nazis he's working with begins to worry as Ezra starts to unravel their plot. The order is shut down. Not knowing this, he attacks one of his assassins for not carrying out his duty. He's informed, however, that his Nazi higher-ups have decided to abort the mission. They burn down Mengele's home in Brazil and kill all the people who work on the property. Mengele strikes out on his own.

He heads off to Pennsylvania, where one of the hits is scheduled. He meets up with a man named Wheelock, who adopted one of the cloned Hitler children, who is named Bobby. Mengele convinces Wheelock to lock up his Dobermans, claiming he's afraid of dogs. He then shoots the man dead.

Mengele was posing as Ezra, who is en route to the farm.

When he arrives, he instantly recognizes Mengele and attacks him. The two men struggle, with Ezra keeping up the fight even after he's been shot. Mengele manages to get the best of Ezra and holds his gun on him. Ezra lunges to the door keeping the dogs back and lets them in. They attack Mengele, but Bobby comes home and calls them off.

Ezra and Mengele both talk to Bobby, Mengele trying to convince Bobby that he is the good guy. Bobby picks up that the dogs must have attacked Mengele because he had a weapon. Ezra convinces Bobby to go look for his father, who Mengele has left in the basement since killing him. Bobby finds the man, comes out and orders the dogs to attack Mengele. They tear him apart, with Bobby apparently taking some sadistic pleasure in it.

Bobby considers letting Ezra die, but then agrees to send for help when Ezra promises he won't contact the police about what happened. Ezra makes it to the hospital and is met by Bennett, a member of a radical Jewish organization that, like Ezra, hunts ex-Nazis. Unlike Ezra, the organization Bennett works for has no trouble assassinating them.

Ezra managed to get a list of names of the remaining boys. Bennett asks for it, intending to expose the work or, if necessary, assassinate all of the boys on the list. Ezra protests that the boys are innocent children and burns the list.

A short epilogue shows Bobby in a darkroom developing prints of Mengele's bloody death, taking some pleasure in it.

Close to the Truth

There were, of course, many Nazi officers who managed to escape the Allied forces after the end of World War II. As Ezra blandly states in the film, it was widely known that many of them fled to South America. Unlike many conspiracy films, this one starts from an established conspiracy—the conspiracy to hide Nazi war criminals—and builds on it to create its fiction.

Mengele actually did live in South America following the war. He was in Allied custody for a time, but the chaos following the surrender of Germany was such that they let him go before realizing who they had. He lived underground for over 30 years, moving from Argentina to Paraguay and then on to Brazil, where he died from drowning when he suffered a stroke while swimming. It took until the 1980s to find and positively identify his remains. In the 1990s, further DNA testing verified that the remains were Mengele's. *The Boys from Brazil* was released in October of 1978. Mengele died in 1979 at the age of 67.

The SS maintained a network of higher ranking officers who helped several of their organization escape following the war and South America was a popular destination. Documents released in the early 2000s revealed, for instance, that the CIA was aware that Adolf Eichmann was living in Argentina, but that the CIA also failed to go after him in deference to the West Germans, who feared that the infamous Nazi would reveal damaging information about a high ranking German official, Hans Globke, who worked for the Nazis during the war. Heinz Felfe, another wanted SS war criminal, worked for the US intelligence agency in West Germany and, at the same time, provided information to the USSR.

The Boys from Brazil is truly chilling because, while the premise of Mengele's cloning plan might be far-fetched, the idea of Nazi war criminals living out their lives in South America, or even working for current governments, is not far-fetched at all. It's a fact.

The Fiction and Conspiracy Element

The Boys from Brazil uses Mengele in a way that is consistent with his interests in real life. He was obsessed with twins and with people who had two different eye colors. He had an MD and a Ph.D. and was widely reviled for the cruel and unscientific experiments he carried out on patients. He oftentimes murdered patients so that he could conduct autopsies and examine their remains. In short, he was every bit as evil and sadistic—even more so, actually—as portrayed in this film.

The Nazi organization he worked for has not lost sight of its goal and, in fact, the members speak of a Fourth Reich. They still want to take over the world and, despite being among the most wanted men on the planet, they have the power to do it. Part of the conspiracy element in this film that really makes it work is that Mengele is ordered to stop his experiment by his superiors, implying that there are even higher ranking Nazis in other places in the world and that their command structure, though not part of an operating army, is still very much intact.

Ezra is based on a real-life Nazi hunter named Simon Wiesenthal. Wiesenthal tracked down several Nazi war criminals and, like Ezra in the movie, he did pursue Mengele, but never managed to catch him. At one point, he offered a $100,000 reward for the capture of the doctor.

The conspiracy theory in this film extends the real conspiracy—simply escaping prosecution—to include a plot to bring about the rise of the Nazi movement once again. The Mengele portrayed in the film is not only unrepentant, but is still convinced of the importance of his mission.

Many conspiracy films ask us to imagine shadowy figures behind real events or to accept a completely fictionalized villain. In *The Boys from Brazil*, the conspirators might be fictionalized, but they are based on very real and very dangerous people, some of whom were part of a conspiracy that thwarted some of the best intelligence agencies in the world for decades. Others ascended to heights of power that allowed them to keep on operating essentially in the open, with their crimes and associations with the Nazis actually sheltering them from being captured and tried for what they'd done.

Enjoying this Paranoid Thriller

The Boys from Brazil has some of the best actors to ever appear on screen among its cast. It has a tight, fast-moving plot that keeps things focused at all times. We get a great character in Ezra and, with him as our guide, get to uncover the conspiracy step by step. The film currently has good ratings from critics and fans alike, and there are very good reasons for that aside from the aforementioned.

In some of these thrillers, you'll see yourself dragged through incredibly complex plots. In some cases, names and dates are dropped in rapid succession, implying that there's some sort of connection between them and whatever event is believed to have been the work of a conspiracy. This film avoids that.

The Boys from Brazil gives us three things we need to make a movie work right from the start: a protagonist we like, an antagonist we don't like and a plot for the audience to follow. It's a well-written story. Despite the many players in the conspiracy and the breadth of it—it literally spans decades—the film tells the story in very direct terms and never becomes hard to follow. We're given a lot of information and a lot of characters, but the movie does not lose the audience in the details. The main thrust of the story always remains apparent: Josef Mengele wants to clone Hitler and Ezra is going to stop him.

Some critics felt that the performances were a bit over the top.

The criticism seems a bit odd, however, given the characters being portrayed. Peck plays Mengele, one of the most murderous, genuinely evil figures of the 20th century. Mengele's reputation and his successful flight from being held accountable from it make him an enormously significant historical figure. It's hard to see how one could play him subtly. He's essentially evil incarnate, and Peck comes through in portraying that. Everything about the man is elegant and refined on the surface, but cold as ice inside. He's at once completely driven to complete his task but utterly empty as a human being.

Ezra, played by Lawrence Olivier, is very likeable and, given his advanced age at the time of the film, comes off as something of a sweet old man. He's kind-hearted, very loving and respectful with his wife and everyone he deals with. He's a very engaging character, and about as smart as they come. He's also incredibly tenacious. Like Mengele, he's driven to the point of his life being defined by his mission, but he's on the right side of history and humanity. When he does encounter Mengele, we see a fight between two old men long past their primes, but the hatred is visceral. Ezra takes a shot to the chest and keeps on coming. The way this scene is pulled off, even at this man's very advanced age, you see the toughness that made him a survivor. He doesn't die easily and he doesn't forget a wrong. At the end of the film, however, we see that, in dancing with the devil for so long, he has not become a devil himself and he gives the clones of one of the most evil figures in history a chance to define themselves as people rather than judging them based on where they came from.

This movie is well worth watching, more than once. It's got all the elements of a great conspiracy thriller but doesn't have to establish just how dangerous the prey that Ezra is hunting really is. This makes it truly tense at times. Jeremy Black, the actor who plays the Boys themselves, is chilling as well, and makes the film even better for his work as the cloned Hitler children.

Coma (1978)

Director:

Michael Crichton

Starring:

Elizabeth Ashley

Geneviève Bujold

Michael Douglas

Rip Torn

Coma takes the paranoia out of the realm of international espionage and places it right in your doctor's office. This simple but effective thriller has a dark, sinister feel to it throughout and a well-rendered conspiracy story at its core.

The Plot

Dr. Susan Wheeler is a promising surgical resident. She and her boyfriend, Dr. Mark Bellows, work at Boston Memorial Hospital. Susan has to not only tackle the challenges of being a doctor, but the sexism she deals with at work and at home.

Wheeler and Bellows open up the film having a fight. Susan talks to her friend about it at a dance class the next day, after Susan and Mark make up. Her friend reveals that she's having an abortion at the hospital and that she doesn't want her husband to find out, so the operation is being reported as being done for irregular menstrual cycles. Susan assures her friend that the operation is routine and nothing to worry about.

During the operation, the anesthesiologist starts getting distressing readings from Susan's friend. She ends up brain dead, though she was a healthy, young woman who was undergoing a routine procedure.

Susan is disturbed by the incident so she looks into how many patients have been discharged in a comatose state from Boston Memorial. She finds the list disturbingly long. The head surgeon at the hospital, Dr. George Harris, finds out that Susan pulled the patient records, which causes a stir. In doing so, Susan violated privacy regulations. Harris is annoyed with her and implies that it would be sad to lose a promising young surgeon.

Susan isn't satisfied with the explanations she's given, all of which are very hazy and imply that it just happens, basically. She goes down to the pathology lab and starts talking to the pathologists about how one might induce a coma deliberately, and in a way that cannot be detected. They point to a drug that the anesthesiologists use and carbon monoxide. One of the pathologists remarks that carbon monoxide makes the blood very red, so anyone performing a surgery wouldn't have cause to think that the patient was suffering from a lack of oxygen.

Susan finds out that the comatose patients are being taken to the Jefferson Institute for care. She visits the institute with Mark, but isn't allowed in. She's encouraged to come back for a prearranged tour later in the week.

Susan continues to investigate what's going on. Mark makes

her feel like she's being paranoid. Eventually, as she's leaving a surgery, a maintenance man talks to her on the sly. He tells her to come down to the basement. He knows where they have the tank of CO stashed and how the system works and offers to help Susan.

Susan goes down to meet the maintenance man but walks in after a hitman has already killed the maintenance man, making it look like and accident. Susan finds the CO system, however, and traces its route up to operating room eight, where every incident where someone went into a coma started.

The hitman is after Susan soon enough. She manages to evade him, blinding him temporarily with a fire extinguisher and pushing him down a flight of stairs. He continues chasing her, with Susan leading him down to an area of the hospital where they store cadavers. She manages to ambush the hitman, dropping several bodies on him and escaping.

Susan runs to Mark's house to tell him what's going on. He doesn't believe her, but offers her some valium. Susan hears him talking to someone on the phone and saying that he'll keep her there. Afraid that Mark's in on it, she runs away.

Susan gets into the Jefferson Institute as part of the tour. She finds the facility full of comatose patients. They're suspended from the ceiling by wires to prevent bed sores. A computerized system takes action by changing their position or their life support when needed. Susan sneaks off and explores. She overhears a conversation between two surgeons talking about auctioning off organs from the comatose patients.

We learn that the Jefferson Institute is holding auctions over the phone with hospitals around the world. The organs they harvest go to the highest bidder. Susan manages to escape the security at the Institute and goes back to Boston Memorial.

Back at Boston Memorial, she goes to tell Dr. Harris what she's found out. They have a scotch together and she realizes that Dr. George Harris is actually the same person she'd heard referred to as Dr. George at the Institute. Before she can do anything, however, she realizes that Dr. Harris has also drugged her. The drug mimics appendicitis, and Dr. Harris is going to perform her appendectomy, in operating room eight.

Susan comes around enough to let Mark know that she's been drugged. She hits his pager surreptitiously, giving him an excuse to get out of being in on the operation. Mark goes to the basement and finds the CO line and the radio-controlled switching device that activates it.

During the operation, Susan starts to show the same signs that the other victims showed, but pulls through. As she awakes from the anesthesia, Dr. Harris's face drops. Susan is wheeled out of the operating room. We see police officers waiting outside the OR; Dr. Harris turns off the x-ray viewer and the film ends.

Keeping it Simple Makes it Work

Films and television shows that feature medical professionals tend to have a lot of technical language thrown into their scripts. It adds realism and, for the part of the audience that is in the know about such things, it adds depth. *Coma* is no exception in this regard. We get plenty of long medication names, procedure names and so forth. The film, however, manages to keep what needs to be simple as simple as possible, and it makes the conspiracy a lot easier to follow.

Once we're out of the medical jargon, the pilot is very straight-forward. Someone is inducing comas in perfectly healthy patients. Those patients end up at the Jefferson Institute. The Jefferson Institute is set up to keep comatose patients alive for as long as possible but, at the same time, it's a very easy place for someone to die without anyone asking any questions. Using that, a group of organ thieves is selling transplant organs to the highest bidder and the highest levels of authority at Boston Memorial are in on the plot.

This conspiracy is no labyrinth of players and interests as we might see in a paranoid political thriller, but it's remarkably effective. It's easy enough to understand that the audience can concentrate on the action in the film and the characters, both of which are very well done.

Susan the Protagonist

Susan is a great character. She's a career woman in the late 1970s, so she faces a lot of sexism. It seems as though everyone challenges everything she says at some level. When she discovers something very wrong at the hospital, she is dismissed as being paranoid or emotional. That's not the worst rub of the movie. Whether it's intentional or not, *Coma* gives some insight into what women of Susan's generation put up with.

When Mark and Susan get back to their apartment at the beginning of the film, Mark wants Susan to get him a beer and make supper. He says he's had a very long and hard day. Susan, however, has had a very long and hard day as well. She hops in the shower and tells Mark to take care of it himself. It ends up starting an argument. Mark is more or less unwilling to show Susan the same amount of respect that he insists that she shows him. He brings up hospital politics, saying that someone has to be interested in it, since Susan isn't.

Susan isn't interested in politics at all. She's interested in her job and, by all indications in this film, she's very good at it.

As Susan investigates the conspiracy further, she shows a great deal of courage, which the plot necessitates. She also, however, shows a great capacity for quick, rational thinking, which makes the character very likeable. When she needs to know how to put someone in a coma, she visits the pathologists. The pathologists even admit that, if you want to know how to kill someone and get away with it, they're the people to ask.

Susan then gets information from the maintenance man who gives her insight into how the mechanical elements of the murder weapon—such as it is—work. Finding the man dead and getting chased by a hitman later on, she does brilliantly, using information she got from the real security guard to confirm that the man posing as him is fake.

Susan's character is one that very much demands respect. She shouldn't have to ask for it, but oftentimes does. She's a bit more perceptive than her fellow doctors, for certain, not accepting their excuses for people going into comas during routine procedures. This is a woman who is obviously not averse to challenging the power structure, and that helps her to figure out the cause of the comas and, in the process, to save lives.

Susan is a person who notices problems where others ignore them and who sees solutions when she's under pressure. She's a great female lead for films of this era and *Coma* does the viewer the service of giving her some very intimidating enemies to go up against. Her investigation into the mishaps at the hospital is completely believable, as she simply does what any good scientist or doctor does. They look at the evidence, see where the data points and figure out a suitable explanation, and then test it.

Very Effective Dread
Many of the films in these books are about people being pur-

sued by shady government agencies, or by conspiracies within those agencies. On a certain level, an intelligence agency is expected to operate in the shadows. Not so doctors, and this film plays on that fact to make a very tense story.

Those who are in on the conspiracy in this film do their killing when their victims are at their most vulnerable. In political paranoid thrillers, the protagonist is usually on the run from a well-equipped, experienced and ruthless organization, but can also make a run for it, fight back and resist their pursuer in other ways. These conspirators are masters of murdering for profit and being completely untraceable. They favor the healthy and the young for their organs and, no matter how fast, smart or dangerous someone is, they're vulnerable when a surgeon is working on them. Nobody is really safe if they end up in operating room eight. If some government assassin is after you, you could presumably run far enough or fast enough to get away from them. Everyone, however, needs medical care at some point, and a conspiracy among those who provide it is really quite disturbing.

Enjoying this Paranoid Thriller

Coma is only one of the really great paranoid thrillers that came out in the 1970s. Because of Watergate, presumably, most of the thrillers of this era involve government and military/industrial conspiracies. This one offers something a bit different than those. For people who don't really care for films that deal with espionage, politics and related themes, *Coma* is perfect.

The film is part murder mystery and a great deal of the film is spent showing Susan figuring out the plan, who's involved in it and why it exists in the first place. There's a lot more darkness here than the average mystery story, however, and some of the shots—morgues, bland yet sinister hospital hallways, empty basements and tunnels—are almost horror movie like in their construction. There's a real sense of danger at the hospital, and the way the shots are constructed and lit makes it even more visceral.

The film's protagonist is also an interesting one for this genre. She's not a fish-out-of-water character, like Dustin Hoffman in *Marathon Man*. She lives in the same world as the conspirators. Conversely, she's not like Redford's character in *Three Days of the Condor*, who had at least some training to help him deal with situations where his life was in danger. Susan's able to understand how the conspirators work and why, but she has to rely on quick thinking and intelligence to get herself out of the worst situations.

This film is certainly full of paranoia. Susan seems like she's getting pushed a bit too far for her to handle at times, and she does incorrectly suspect some people in her life of being part of the conspiracy who aren't. Then again, Susan really is on to something; it's a frightening plot and it's great to watch her figure it all out.

Coma was remade recently, but this 1978 original still holds up and is an effective paranoid thriller.

Blow Out (1981)

Director:

Brian De Palma

Starring:

John Travolta

Nancy Allen

Blow Out is a straightforward but good thriller involving a political conspiracy that centers on an assassination. With loose ends to tie up, an audio engineer and a woman who was involved in a blackmail plot find themselves targets of a ruthless assassin.

The Plot
Blow Out opens up with a film-within-a-film sequence. Jack Terry is watching a film along with its director. It's a cheap slasher, full of sorority girls getting stabbed by a stalker. Terry is a sound effects technician. The director gets annoyed with him using too many library sounds on his films and tells him to go out and get some ambient sounds.

Terry goes to a park and starts recording the ambient sounds. As he's getting audio footage, he sees a car accident. A car goes off a bridge and into the water below. He manages to swim out and save a female passenger, but the man is dead by the time he gets there.

The dead man was the governor. The governor had been gaining momentum as a presidential candidate. He was riding with Sally, who was a call girl. While he's still in the hospital, a man working for the governor tells Jack to forget about what happened.

Jack meets Sally in the hospital and seems taken with her.

When Jack plays back his audio footage, he finds something odd. Right before the sound of the blowout and the wreck, there's a sound that seems to be a gunshot. He listens to the tape over and over.

When Jack's watching the news, a man comes on who said he was filming at the time of the accident and caught everything on film. His film is published in a magazine. The filmmaker, Karp, doesn't put all of the stills from his film in the magazine, but Jack manages to edit together an animation of them that he can sync up with his audio.

As he reviews the footage, Jack gets more confirmation of his theory when he spots an apparent muzzle flash in the frame at the same time the audio captured a gunshot.

Sally was actually working for Karp when he made the film. The man behind the film was the assassin who fired the bullet in the frame. As Jack starts to figure out what's going on, he realizes that Sally is a loose end. She was supposed to have died in the wreck as well.

The hitman talks to his employers and tells them he's going to kill Sally and make it look like a serial killer's work. He kills some women beforehand, choosing them because they look somewhat like Sally.

A local newscaster tries to get Jack to tell his story. Jack sends Sally off with a wire to meet with the media, but realizes that the man he thought was showing up is not there. He goes after the hitman, who gets Sally to go down to a subway tunnel and then takes her to a nearby Liberty Day celebration. Jack gets in a car crash trying to catch them, wakes up in an ambulance and continues his chase. The hitman drags Sally up on a roof and tries to kill her. Jack doesn't manage to save her, but manages to get a hold of the hitman and stab him to death.

The conspiracy hasn't any loose ends left, so it goes unacknowledged. Jack goes back to work on the slasher film.

A Morbid Twist
There's a subplot in this film that involves Jack trying to find the perfect scream for a shower murder sequence in the slasher film. Throughout the movie, it's referenced again and again, and Jack is tasked with getting more realistic sound.

Before Sally gets taken in by the hitman, Jack wires her so he can record any audio that might reveal the entire conspiracy. When Sally gets killed, she lets out a very authentic scream, of course, which ends up getting used in the film. It's a rather morbid part of the story, but it's also darkly comic. Jack can't listen to the scream at the end of the film.

Good and Paranoid
This film has some obvious grounding in real life events. The government cover-up theme is very Watergate. The death of the governor has some similarities to the Chappaquiddick car wreck, but this film doesn't try to serve as an allegory for either of them.

This film uses the events to spin a pretty standard, but very effective, conspiracy story. The hitman, the implication that the conspiracy goes very high up and the one person who knows the truth but who can't seem to convince anyone of what's really go on are all common to the story form. Travolta is very good in this film, however, and he's given enough of a character to make it interesting.

Jack is something of a conspiracy nut, at least when he latches on to the fact that he's stumbled upon a real life conspiracy. He gets obsessed and, as he admits, some of what he's discovering could be done through lab processes. There's always a bit of doubt about whether Jack is going overboard, but the audio recording doesn't lie. There is definitely the sound of a gunshot in that audio footage.

Of course, it all gets taken away from him at one point. Destroying the evidence is always one of the primary goals of any conspiracy and this film makes sure to include that. It makes Jack look completely paranoid. When he drops off an audio and video reel to someone he knows at the police department, it turns out to be completely blank. It does a good job of destroying Jack's credibility, also a common tactic of conspiracies and the people who protect them.

All the elements are here. This film isn't particularly innovative with the story, but the way it's told is. It does show that, even with technology far less advanced than what most people have in their homes today, it's easy enough to doctor evidence. Jack is doing things right. He's trying to take what media of the crash he has and piece it together in some way that makes sense. When he does so, signs point to a conspiracy.

It makes the story interesting, because it leaves open the possibility that Jack is just fooling himself. It's not unusual to hear a gunshot or something that sounds very much like one in any city on any given night. Jack could be going over the top with his paranoia, but the film proves him right in most regards, and allows the conspiracy to win, ultimately giving it a darker edge.

Enjoying this Paranoid Thriller

Blow Out is definitely worth seeing for fans of paranoid thrillers in general. It's a dark film, but the fact that it's not meant to too heavily reference any real life cover-ups or conspiracies makes it a bit more escapist than some of the other films in this book.

The film is well acted and well made. The story stays focused and it keeps moving forward. There are some subplots here and there—Jack's background as a sound tech for law enforcement, for instance—that add something to the characters and make it feel like more than a formula paranoid thriller.

This film isn't quite as well known as some of the other thrillers of its era, but it's one of the better ones, for certain. It's very effective in where it takes the viewer and has plenty of great twists and turns that keep it intelligent and engaging.

They Live (1988)

Director:

John Carpenter

Starring:

Keith David

Meg Foster

Roddy Piper

As far as paranoid thrillers that are fun go, it's hard to beat *They Live*. A combination of conspiracy film, 80s action flick and sci-fi horror, this film doesn't take itself too seriously and has some very memorable moments.

The Plot
Piper plays our protagonist, John, who is an average guy who works construction. He and Frank, another worker, strike up a friendship. Like John, Frank is a big, intimidating guy but nice overall.

John notices that there are some strange things going on. He sees a man screaming for people to wake up and there seem to be signs that people are getting paranoid everywhere. Pirate broadcasts warn of some sort of a conspiracy and people get headaches while watching them.

John explores an old church and finds it full of high-tech equipment. He also finds a box, but gets chased away before he can take it. The police come in and break up the homeless village that John is living in. John goes back into the church and finds all of the equipment has been removed, but he finds the box. It's full of sunglasses. He takes a pair and hides the rest.

When John puts on the sunglasses, he sees an entirely different landscape. Billboards change so that, in place of the advertisements that they normally display, they display messages such as "Obey", "Marry and Reproduce" and other such directives. The entire world seems to be filled with messages designed to control people's behavior. Every page of the magazines that John picks up is full of subliminal messages.

John also sees that many of the people around him aren't who they appear to be on the surface. Intermixed with the human population are what appear to be aliens. They have skull-like features with bulging eyes. They don't seem to realize that John can see them at first, until John points out that two people who appear the same to everyone else in a store are, in fact, very different. He insults one of the aliens and runs out of the store.

He gets attacked by the police, who try to reason with him. It ends in a gun fight and John takes the shotgun from their patrol car. He heads to a bank and goes on a rampage.

He starts to see how the aliens operate. They talk through their wristwatches and seem to use them to disappear as well. He kidnaps a television station director and makes her drive him to her house. She doesn't believe John's story, but goes along with him to avoid being hurt.

Holly, the director, manages to get rid of John. He manages to recover the rest of the sunglasses he stashed and finds one of his coworkers, Frank. He tries to get Frank to put on the sunglasses. John, however, is wanted and Frank wants nothing to do with him. The two get into a vicious fight about the glasses. John eventually manages to get Frank to put on the glasses and Frank sees what's going on around him.

Soon enough, the pair hooks up with a group that's resisting the aliens. The sunglasses, which are giving the men migraines, are replaced with contact lenses. The resistance reveals the alien plan. The aliens are warming up the planet with engineered climate change. They're also planning on exploiting every resource on the planet until it's used up.

The resistance gives Frank and John some supplies. Holly also shows up. The police arrive shortly after and attack the meeting. Using one of the alien wristwatches, Frank and John manage to get out of the meeting without getting shot, but end up in the alien complex, which is located underground.

There they run into humans who are colluding with the aliens, all of them celebrating their successful ventures together at a party. One of the collaborators gives Frank and John the information on the entire enterprise. He shows how the aliens are getting to Earth and other planets and how they've hooked right into the television networks. The signal that prevents anyone from seeing the aliens as they really are emanates from Chanel 54, where Holly works.

John and Frank decide to destroy the transmitter. They shoot the alien guard in the television station and battle their way up to the transmitter. Holly returns and manages to kill Frank. She confronts John on the roof and gets him to drop his gun. A helicopter full of aliens is aiming at John at the same time, however he manages to pull a gun and shoot Holly. He then shoots up the equipment broadcasting the signal before the aliens in the helicopter kill him.

The signal gone, the aliens are clearly visible for what they are, ending the deception.

Not too Subtle

This film came out toward the end of the Reagan years and it's not too subtle in terms of using the aliens as metaphors. The director himself said that the aliens were basically Reagan Republicans. It's a bit of a departure from the way that conspiracies are portrayed in the Nixon/Watergate era thrillers of the 70s, but it's done in a way that makes this movie a lot of fun.

John is basically any working class person. The characters in this film talk about factories shutting down and taking sledgehammers to their rich managers' cars. They talk about the unfairness of life. In the homeless shanty town where John first gets set up, the people are poor and desperate, but genuine. They're good people. The wealthy people are creepy aliens with skull faces who put subliminal messages into everything. They want people to breed, obey and consume. It's basically corporate, Wall Street, conformist America at its worst and Carpenter makes no secret of how he feels about all of it.

Under their veneer, these wealthy, powerful people are all ugly. They're hideous, in fact, and they're all working together to keep everyone else stupid, ill informed, titillated and obedient. A street preacher is one of the few in this film who know the truth. He and the other members of the resistance against the aliens are targets, naturally, and the murderousness of the alien enterprise is exposed in how the aliens deal with those who know about them or, worse, oppose them openly.

The conspiracy here is a variation on the famous Wilde line

about the gods punishing us by answering our prayers. If you work with the aliens, you get whatever you want. You get money, power, access and a sense of importance. It's the kind of benefit package that people will kill to preserve, as Holly demonstrates. In order to have all that, however, somebody has to suffer, and that somebody would be John and the people like him.

Not subtle at all, but it's effective. The film actually manages to avoid being preachy and to be a lot of fun and, at times, hilarious.

The Memorable Parts

This is one of the most famous appearances of Roddy Piper, who had a very long career as a professional wrestler and who continues to appear in films and television programs. This film is not a thinking person's paranoid thriller, but it's excellent. It has very good reviews and while some critics heaped scorn upon it, others described it as "engaging", and there are, indeed, some very engaging things about this film.

Piper has some very cheesy lines in this film. Rather than trying to make them sound serious or playing them up in a way that makes them groan-worthy, he delivers them perfectly. They sound like the kinds of things that John would say, given what else we know about him. John isn't the sharpest tool in the shed, to be sure, but he's a good guy. When he starts insulting the aliens for being ugly and says that he came into a bank to chew bubblegum and kick ass—and is all out of bubble gum—it's somehow not at all horrible. Piper makes it funny.

When he says that you can't see the aliens without the "special sunglasses", he makes it sound completely insane, hilarious and sincere at all once. He keeps this up through the entire film, and even the action sequences, despite their flaws, are fun.

Frank and John hip shoot their assault rifles and hit everything they sort-of aim at. The aliens are comically bad shots. John and Frank are not only winging it as far as infiltrating a heavily-guarded facility is concerned, but are also very big guys. It seems like they would have gotten shot even by accident before they made it to the roof.

The fight scene between Frank and John is another classic moment from this film. It's brutal, but brutal in the way that a professional wrestling match—probably not a coincidence—is brutal. Everything looks horribly painful, but no one gets hurt that badly. Of course, given the size of these men, anyone would have been in the hospital after sustaining the kind of beating both of them handed to one another. It's a hilarious, sometimes cringe-inducing scene, however, and it's one of the best moments in this film.

Holly is a great variation/parody of the female helper character in these films. Many of them have a woman involved who is coerced at one point or another into helping the protagonist and who comes to believe in him after getting to spend some time with him, and maybe sleep with him. Holly almost throws herself at John, but he doesn't really want anything other than some temporary shelter while he figures things out. She does a great job of being condescending; all the while knowing that everything John is saying is true, given that she's a part of it all.

The action sequences in this film are pure 1980s in their style. They do the job and are fun enough, but they're not as intense and certainly not as gory as the action scenes that are popular these days.

The best scenes in this film are really those when John puts on the sunglasses for the first time. The world turns black and white. Everything around him is telling him to shop, breed and remain asleep and obedient. It's a heavy handed message, but it fits. When a politician—who is really an alien—is shown on television talking about how we all need to be optimistic and how it's a new day in America, it's really not a stretch to figure out who the alien is standing in for.

This film is one that action, horror, conspiracy and thriller fans are likely to enjoy equally. It has plenty of memorable moments in it and, in fact, is one of Carpenter's better films.

Enjoying this Paranoid Thriller

Many of the films featured in this book are very serious ones. They've got plots that are analogies for real life conspiracies or, in some cases, purport to tell the truth behind real life conspiracies. In some cases, they're just very dark and hard to forget because of that.

They Live is something different. It's got plenty of social commentary in it, but it's something more than that in that the message in this film isn't necessarily what's on the surface, appropriately enough.

This film shows that when you strip consumer culture down to its essentials, it's ugly and primitive. It's about reproducing and the strong dominating the weak, so they suffer in poverty but are still expected to consume so they can keep the awful engine of their own oppression running. Not only that but it all benefits a very wealthy few, who are as ugly as the culture itself when you strip away their surface trappings.

One of the ways that the tactics the aliens employ are popularly described seems to miss some of the point. The obvious way to describe what the aliens are up to involves subliminal messages. The popular perception that you can use subliminal messages to influence people's behaviors is the result of a hoax. While the technique may be bunk, the notion is a powerful one, and this film plays on that, but it also touches on something even more powerful.

In the film, John puts on the special sunglasses and sees a billboard advertising travel with an image of a shapely female leg on a beach that actually encourages the viewer to reproduce. This is subliminal? The shapely leg seems obvious enough in what it implies. Shop signs read "Consume." Again, this isn't really subliminal so much as just saying the exact same thing in different terms. Every shop sign is encouraging passersby to consume. Every advertisement that shows attractive bodies is invoking sex and romance. Every political magazine is asking you to accept and obey something or someone.

What's interesting here is that the sunglasses don't show the hidden messages, they just distill them. It's more about efficiency than it is about truth. The world even turns black and white when John puts the sunglasses on. Everything is an in-your-face message, though most of those messages are essentially the same when John takes the glasses off. Obey, consume, marry and reproduce, stay asleep, watch TV: these are all messages we get in overt forms every day.

This film is about taking down pretense, which is the real conspiracy here. The conspiracy is really one of keeping people stupid by feeding them exactly what they want and slowly stripping the economy, the working people and even the planet of all it could offer and all the ways each could be made better.

They Live is really one of the better paranoid thrillers out there as far as entries that aren't particularly dark are concerned. It's witty, fun and has a good time poking fun at the Reagan-era and the dumbly-smiling optimism of the 80s. Those who fancy themselves non-conformists will likely very much enjoy this film, as will conspiracy theorists who want something a bit lighter, but still very effective, to enjoy.

JFK (1991)

Director:

Oliver Stone

Starring:

Gary Oldman

Kevin Bacon

Kevin Costner

Laurie Metcalf

Sissy Spacek

Tommy Lee Jones

JFK could well be the mother of all JFK conspiracy thrillers. This movie, clocking in at well over 3 hours in length, goes through just about every single JFK conspiracy during its runtime. It's source material for those who are obsessed with the assassination and still compelling drama for those who find the conspiracy theories surrounding the event to be complete flights of fancy.

The Plot
This film starts out with a montage of historical footage, setting up the viewer for the narrative. We see Dwight Eisenhower giving his farewell address in 1961. This is the address where

he famously introduced the term "military-industrial complex" into the American vernacular and where he warned the nation not to let it get too much power. We're then taken forward in time to a synopsis of the Kennedy administration. Kennedy symbolized youth, the change of the old order and the introduction of new ideas.

We're given a narrative that portrays Kennedy at dangerous odds with the military-industrial complex, giving us plenty of reasons to assume that he had ruthless and powerful enemies.

The Kennedy assassination and a great deal of footage related to it follow. We're shown how strongly he divided the nation in the days following the assassination. Two men at the same bar, between them, both celebrate and lament the assassination.

Jim Garrison, a district attorney in New Orleans, finds out that there are connections between the people named in the assassination and New Orleans. He investigates David Ferrie, who has connections to anti-communist groups. He starts noticing things about Lee Harvey Oswald that don't seem to make sense. Before he can do anything with the information, however, the investigation is closed down. Lee Harvey Oswald is killed by Jack Ruby and there is no way to continue forward with the case.

Years later, Garrison is still curious about the inconsistencies with the case and starts pouring over the Warren Report. He goes through the testimony line by line, finding places where obvious questions were never asked and noticing contradictory evidence.

Garrison wants to get the bottom of it and recruits associates to help him who he believes will fight to find out the truth. He looks into the connections between Ferrie and Oswald and Ruby. He eventually tracks down a male prostitute, Willie, who is currently incarcerated. He interviews Willie at the prison and, with nothing left to lose, Willie offers to tell him everything he knows.

Willie had a client named Clay Bertrand. While partying with him one night, he heard Bertrand and Ferrie talking about killing the president. He also reports having met Oswald.

More evidence of a conspiracy starts to pop up. A witness who claimed she saw someone firing from the grassy knoll claims that the Secret Service intimidated her, telling her what story to tell just after the assassination happened.

Garrison decides to run a practical test on the Warren Report's theory. He and one of his staffers go up to the book depository and attempt to mimic the same shots that Oswald is claimed to have gotten off. They determine that it would have been impossible for Oswald to have fired three shots within the slightly more than 5 seconds the report claims.

Garrison journeys to Washington. There he meets an intelligence operative who only gives the name "X", but who gives Garrison a great deal of the information that he's after. In a 15-minute monologue, X spins a conspiracy theory that involves everyone from the Mafia to weapons manufacturers to the vice president—and president at the time—himself. The wide-ranging conspiracy implies that Kennedy wanted to get out of Vietnam and that he was attacking the power of the CIA. The military-industrial complex being thus threatened, they launched the conspiracy to kill the president. X implicates Clay Shaw, who is located in New Orleans, as part of the conspiracy and tells Garrison to go after him.

Shaw is brought in and gives the name Clay Bertrand as one of his aliases. He is, however, quickly set free. He claims he knows nothing of the conspiracy or the conspirators.

Garrison decides to bring Shaw in on charges of conspiracy to murder the president and to put him on trial.

Meanwhile, Garrison's personal life starts to go down the tubes. His family starts to fall apart because of his obsession with the case. His daughter gets a call one night claiming that her dad entered her in a beauty contest and she won. She's asked when she gets off of school and other personal information by the caller before her mother hangs up the line.

Garrison starts to see evidence that he's being targeted by the conspiracy. Watching the news one night, he sees a report that makes false accusations about his methods and that attacks his character. His witnesses start to back out, he loses staff members and Ferrie turns up dead.

Garrison pushes forward, even after one of his own staff members is revealed to be working with the conspirators and shares information that compromises Garrison's case. He lays out the entire conspiracy theory, keeping the jury entranced. He manages to implicate everyone up to President Johnson in the conspiracy along the way and gives a rousing speech about the meaning of a free country.

Nonetheless, the jury finds Shaw innocent of the charges. The film states at the end that the documents related to the Kennedy assassination will be released in 2029, though they were mostly released early due to the impact of this film.

Courting Controversy

JFK raised more than a bit of controversy when it was released, and even before it came out in theaters. Predictably, the controversy was mostly over the historical accuracy of the film. It does present a compelling narrative and, because it is so well made, it tends to lend an air of credibility to its theories.

One of the most important premises of the film is that JFK was a threat to the military-industrial complex. The film makes several claims that Kennedy wanted to make peace with the communists or, at least, create an environment that could foster peace. It also alleges that Kennedy was trying to take power away from the CIA. The movie hints at all of this—and sometimes very strongly—throughout, but the big moment where the conspiracy is revealed in all its vile gory is when X gives his nearly 15-minute long monologue to Garrison in Washington, revealing all the information and each of the conspirators involved. The film presents all of this very much as if it were irrefutable fact.

The conspiracy theory that X so eloquently reveals, however, is not based in reality. It's based on a hoax called *The Report from Iron Mountain.* In the film, however, this conspiracy theory ties all the major players in the event together and reveals the forces behind it, as well as the motivation for those forces to put their awful plan into action. This conspiracy theory, however, is bunk and its source is well known. Nonetheless, it remains a favorite among conspiracy theorists.

Willie O'Keefe, the homosexual prostitute, is a fictional character. He's based on a man named Perry Russo, according to The Guardian. While *JFK* has a sequence where Garrison is accused of drugging witnesses as a way to destroy his credibility, assumedly by the conspirators, Russo was drugged when he gave his testimony. He was also hypnotized. Garrison, according to the same reporting, was not a homosexual prostitute, but a heterosexual insurance salesman.

In the film, one of the most persuasive moments—if one isn't paying attention closely—is when Garrison and one of his associates go to the book depository and try to recreate Oswald's shots at the president. They conclude that there's no way that Oswald could have fired off the rifle in less than six seconds, as the Warren Report claims. However, even in this scene, it takes them under 6 seconds to do just that. Garrison claims that it takes longer to pull off the shots, but even in the film it doesn't.

One of the other truly compelling pieces of evidence, possibly the most compelling, is revealed in the courtroom scene. This is where the Magic Bullet theory is introduced. It basically holds that, in order to have injured Connally and killed Kennedy, the bullet would have had to have paused in mid-air at one point, changed direction several times and performed other impossible feats. Unfortunately, the information presented in this scene is not true to the forensic evidence from the shooting.

One of the biggest sticking points with the argument that Garrison gives is how it shows Connally and Kennedy sitting in the limo. Connally was not sitting directly in front of the president when he was shot and, in fact, was positioned so that the single bullet theory makes perfect sense.

Gruesome as they may be, there are photos available where you can see the actual bullet wounds themselves. They do not line up with Garrison's theory as told in the film, nor do they indicate that the single bullet would have had to have taken some magical trajectory to do its damage.

There are many other instances such as this one in the film.

When it's implied that Garrison is going after Shaw because Shaw is gay, it's written off as a false charge leveled by the conspirators. In fact, Garrison was very interested in Shaw's sexuality and considered it to be a significant factor in making his case. In fact, Garrison suspected quite a few people he associated with the conspiracy, including Oswald himself, of being homosexuals. Their homosexuality was, according to some of Garrison's theorizing, part of what brought them all together.

There are conflicting portrayals of Garrison. Some sources portray him as a relentless crusader for the truth, as he appears in *JFK*. Others portray him as an obsessive conspiracy theorist with a particular interest in the sexual pastimes of the accused conspirators. Whichever way one views the content of this film, however, the execution is a big part of why it has very high reviews and why it's generally considered to be a great film.

Just Watch the Film

For those who adhere to conspiracy theories surrounding Kennedy's assassination, *JFK* is likely to be one of the most satisfying films imaginable. For those who feel that the conspiracy theories are all bunk, the film is likely to be an exercise in frustration at worst, amusement at best. If one can put aside prejudices, however, the masterful filmmaking on display here is really something to see.

In this film, the characters constantly go through enormously complicated scenarios, oftentimes in rapid-fire speeches. Nonetheless, the film doesn't lose the viewer's interest for a moment. The way that the scenes are written and acted makes them engrossing. The theories oftentimes get so convoluted that it's hard to keep track of who did what to whom or why some random piece of information is supposed to be significant. There are some historical inaccuracies that ratchet up the tension, such as the way that Ferrie dies. Ferrie is shown giving a detailed confession to Garrison right before he died, but Ferrie did no such thing in real life. He maintained that he was innocent.

Even when X comes on screen and goes off on his monologue, it's engrossing. The character goes off on a very complex conspiracy that basically includes every shadowy bad guy organization that conspiracy theorist blame most everything on at some level. When X delivers it, however, it doesn't feel like assumption, conjecture and poor logic. It feels like revelation. Garrison's suspicions are not only confirmed in this scene, they're celebrated.

This scene sets the stage for the movie's biggest moment, Garrison's speech before the jury at Shaw's trial. This speech goes on for roughly 20 minutes and is hypnotic. Kevin Costner has caught some flack over the years for some of his lower quality films and his work in them. The courtroom speech, however, makes it apparent that Costner is really a fine actor, an excellent one even. He delivers the speech with such conviction that it makes you want to believe every word of it. He delivers it not like a DA wanting to nail someone for a conspiracy charge, but like a patriot wanting to save what's left of his country from the people who want to alter it forever. He ranges from giving scientific—but incorrect—information about the shooting to the connections between the players to implicating fascism as the real reason behind the assassination. The film does an incredible job of setting the character up for this speech. When Bobby Kennedy is gunned down, Garrison says that "they" got him. It's clear that he believes that behind the assassination are shadowy forces that need to be exposed. He offers a line about how he feels about justice, that is has to be done though the heavens may fall. This is the sort of great characterization that makes a great film.

Despite its twists and turns, one never forgets that this film is really about Garrison and his hunt to find the truth behind Kennedy's death. It manages to pack a tremendous amount of information into a tremendously long run time and not to lose the viewer's interest.

Just watching this film can be a challenge, however, as the message and the meaning behind it are both very powerful.

Enjoying this Paranoid Thriller

Whether its premise makes you feel vindicated or enraged, you will not be able to deny that *JFK* is a great film. It's one of the best out there in any genre. The performances are excellent all round. The sense of tension is palpable at every twist and turn. One always feels that there is some menace lurking in the shadows and that the protagonist is at the center of it all. This film, over the course of more than 3 hours, never lets you forget what it's really about, and that's saying something.

If you buy into the conspiracy theories, this film really does a great job of laying them out. It does combine several different conspiracy theories into its overall argument, but that's likely to make it only more enjoyable for those who like a good conspiracy film or who like to put time into figuring out whether there were shadowy forces behind Kennedy's murder. You'll have a hard time finding anyone, fictional or real, who can argue these conspiracy theories better than Garrison does in this film. You'll be led astray quite a bit, of course, but that's necessary to the plot of this film and Stone does it masterfully.

If you don't buy into the conspiracy theories, this film is like a study in why people believe them. It casts Kennedy as a real threat to the military-industrial complex, even though that's not borne out by his actions in real life. It implies a range of different conspirators being involved in Kennedy's death, from mobsters to high-ranking military and intelligence personnel, and gives some insight into why people believe these theories.

In short, it masterfully lays out the logic of the conspiracy theorists, or at least the majority of them. While you may find that logic inherently flawed, it's easy to see why so many people find it so compelling. Kennedy may not have been the force for peace and justice that he's shown as in this film, but it certainly does a good job of showing how people felt about him. They found hope in him. There was the potential for real change coming about because he'd been elected president. He stood for something, was eloquent, charismatic and intensely likeable. When he died, the sorrow was overwhelming for most people. A betrayal of the hope he represented.

That, combined with the fact that the official investigation into the assassination is not entirely consistent and that a great deal of information was kept secret, makes Kennedy's death fertile grounds for casual conspiracy theorists, those who are a bit suspicious and those who are utterly paranoid alike.

Stone takes a very bold turn in this film. It doesn't reveal the truth behind the Kennedy assassination, assuming there is any that has not already been disclosed. It reveals the passion that keeps people obsessed with this tragic event. It reveals why people are so driven to find the monsters they believe are really responsible for the assassination and how that colors people's perceptions of everything and anything their government does. It's an incredible film in that regard, and neatly represents how the massive social upheavals, assassinations and Vietnam War all conspired to make the 1960s a breeding ground for paranoia.

This film did have an impact. Partially as a result of the controversy it stirred, the Assassination Records Review Board was formed and released the vast majority of the classified reports from the Warren Commission. The only thing left out of the released material were the income tax returns that were included as part of the original evidence. Perhaps this reveals the best way to enjoy this film.

Put aside the conspiracy theories for a moment and consider what this film really proves. Today's cinematic landscape is populated mostly by commercial vehicles that are designed to make a quick buck at least, to launch a franchise at most. Such films, though some of them are very good in many regards, really have no impact. They're forgotten soon after they're released, in most cases.

JFK is different. This film really doesn't try to make it seem like the conspiracy theories are true. What is passed off as compelling evidence can also be seen as the feverish workings inside Garrison's head. We see the conspiracy unfold precisely because our guide through the movie, Garrison, believes that they exist. We see it all through his eyes—the connections, the coincidences that are too convenient to be coincidences, the allegedly bad shot who managed to hit his target, the inconsistencies in the stories and people attached to the assassination. These are all interesting questions, of course, and many of them are made more so by a bit of historical fudging here and there on the part of the filmmaker.

However, this film really did have a meaningful impact. The distrust and paranoia surrounding the JFK assassination came about not only because of the conspiracy theories surrounding it, but because the government made every move it could to make it seem like they weren't willing to reveal the truth. Documents were classified, facts were hidden, and inconsistencies weren't addressed. This only added fuel to the paranoid fires the event itself lit.

JFK helped introduce a bit of needed transparency to the JFK assassination. Whether or not you think there was a conspiracy involved, the story told here by Stone made it necessary for the government to let the people see the evidence for themselves so they could make their own decisions. Whatever you might think of the conspiracy theory this film puts forward, anyone should find this film worth watching simply because of how powerful it is, and how much influence it ended up having.

The Arrival (1996)

Director:

Ted Twohy

Starring:

Charlie Sheen

Lindsay Crouse

Richard Schiff

Ron Silver

Teri Polo

The Arrival is a smart, tense paranoid thriller that involves alien invasion. It has its weaknesses, but is a good choice for someone looking for a paranoid thriller for the UFO crowd.

The Plot
The Arrival starts out in a logical place, at a SETI (Search for Extra Terrestrial Intelligence) installation where Zane Zaminsky is searching stars systems for signs of radio broadcasts. He hits something that is clearly not random. The signal is coming from Wolf 336. The star, on a cosmic scale, at least, is close, at 14 light years away.

Zane tries to confirm the signal with another station, but cannot get in touch with anyone before it fades. He ends up with less than a minute of recorded signal, but it's compelling.

He takes the signal recording to his boss, Phil Gordon. Gordon is skeptical of the recording. After sparring with Zane over it, he tells Zane that they're going to have to let him go. He offers to pay him a month's salary. Zane has also been blacklisted, so he has to seek work installing satellite dishes.

It's not long before Zane builds his own radio telescope out of consumer satellite dishes. His neighbor, a teenager named Kiki, works with him in his lab. Zane tries to find the signal, which is broadcasting on the FM band, far outside the microwave frequencies that SETI usually scans. He picks up the signal again, but it gets cut out by a Spanish language radio station broadcasting from San Marsol, Mexico.

Zane tries to tell one of his coworkers, but finds EMTs dragging his body out of his house. The cause of death was carbon monoxide poisoning.

Zane decides to go to San Marsol. He's immediately greeted by a local guide who offers to take him to a hotel. He gets the guide to take him to the radio station, which has just burned down.

Zane notices that there is a new power plant operating in the town and meets another American scientist. Ilana, a climatologist, is studying climate change and the power plants like the one that's just opened seem to be accelerating the process.

Ilana's equipment is seized by the authorities. Phil seems to be in two places, with Zane seeing a man who looks exactly like him in San Marsol.

Meanwhile, a man working for Phil puts a device in Zane's attic laboratory. It apparently opens up a sort of black hole, sucking everything in the lab, and a bird outside the house, into it.

Ilana goes back to her hotel. Scorpions fall from the ceiling fan and, after creeping about the room for a while, kill her.

Zane goes out to investigate the power plant. He gets inside, posing as a worker. Taking a hidden elevator, he gets to a lower level where he sees an extraterrestrial. The being steps onto some sort of platform and assumes human form, its backward-facing knees snapping forward to complete the transformation.

Zane sees the apparatus that the aliens are using to increase the levels of CO_2 in the atmosphere. As he's watching the process, an alien sees him and sounds an alarm. Zane uses the alien's own equipment to alter his appearance. He nearly escapes, but the travel guide that took him to the hotel shows up in the elevator. The disguise reacts with him somehow, with the fake skin bubbling and coming off in patches.

Zane manages to get away, but the local authorities dismiss him and accuse him of playing a part in Ilana's murder. He then makes it back to the US and goes to find Phil.

Holding Phil at gunpoint, Zane escorts him outside a JPL building and starts interrogating him. Phil reveals that aliens are secretly working to accelerate climate change. They want to increase the temperature of the earth high enough to wipe out humanity. They also require a warmer environment. Zane reveals that his gun is actually a remote control. He takes a tape he made of the conversation.

Phil dispatches more goons to hunt down Zane. Zane finds out that his equipment has disappeared and decides to go to a radio telescope. From there, he can hijack a satellite signal and broadcast his tape.

He, his girlfriend and Kiki all go the radio telescope. They start the process of broadcasting, but Phil and the aliens show up and stop them. Zane gives Kiki the tape and goes to initiate the broadcast from another location in the building. He gets control of the telescope and gets it lined up, but Kiki refuses to start the broadcast. Kiki is an alien.

Phil gets the tape and comes after Zane and Char. Phil barricades and booby traps the door to his control room with liquid nitrogen. The alliance barge through and the liquid nitrogen freezes them. Zane helps Char to escape and starts trying to retrieve the tape from Phil's body.

Another of the black hole devices is activated and starts pulling the entire laboratory into it. Zane manages to escape, along with Char. Kiki runs away and Zane tells him that he will broadcast the tape.

Afterward, in a television control room, all of the screens switch their programming and start playing the tape that Zane recorded.

A Good Twist on the Alien Invasion

The Arrival does some creative things with the alien invasion narrative. Instead of using some sort of super weapon to wipe out humanity, these aliens are planning on simply doing what we're doing ourselves, but faster and to a much greater degree. By changing the habitat on the planet and wiping out the dominant species, they can have it for themselves.

The film doesn't just assume that the viewer will accept this. Wolf 336 is revealed to be a variable star. Zane's transmission is initially dismissed because it doesn't seem as though life could exist in such a system. However, Zane points out that the star only became variable in the recent past, which means that there could still be life there.

Zane picks up the second signal at his house. He figures out that it's of terrestrial origin, so it means that the aliens are talking back and forth and, apparently, what he heard was one part of a conversation. The problem here, of course, is that the conversation would take 28 years to complete: 14 years for the transmission to reach the star and 14 years for the response to make it back—unless, of course, the aliens weren't talking to their home planet.

The conspiracy angle is played very well here, but there are some lacking points. Some of the sequences have their weak spots. An alien goon from a culture that has technology sufficient to terraform a planet and travel 14 light years across space attacks Zane with a sickle of all things. Not only that, but the sickle barely damages a stack of papers but tears through the side of a fire extinguisher like it was made of paper.

As is the case with many of these films, the point of the film is not the action sequences. The point of the film is what leads up to those sequences and, in this regard, it's pulled off very well. The conspiracy doesn't become so convoluted that it's impossible to follow. Zane doesn't turn out to have incredible alien fighting abilities. He seems like a normal scientist, particularly in that he's primarily driven by curiosity. Something doesn't quite make sense and he wants to know why, and ends up putting himself in quite a bit of danger in the process.

There are plenty of creepy characters in this film, and it upholds some of the conventions of this genre. For instance, when someone appears too conveniently in your life—like a tour guide who just shows up when you arrive in a foreign country—they're probably there for a reason you're not aware of. Fortunately, Zane is pretty adept at being paranoid and he starts to suspect something huge pretty quickly.

Enjoying this Paranoid Thriller

Some alien conspiracy theories tend to cover the same ground over and over again. Places like Roswell are mentioned far too often and, in quite a few instances, the aliens have motives that aren't exactly clear, just sinister.

In this film, the aliens have a clear motive and their plan is actually believable, assuming they have the type of technology that we're asked to accept that they have. At the end of the film, we see that their plan seems to be working out for them.

This film does a good job with the conspiracy angle; Sheen is great as the increasingly frightened and outmatched protagonist and there are nice twists and turns throughout. Some of the twists and turns are obvious by the time they arrive, but that doesn't make them less enjoyable.

For anyone who wants to enjoy some UFO/ET conspiracy thrills, this film is worth checking out.

Conspiracy Theory (1997)

Director:

Richard Donner

Starring:

Julia Roberts

Mel Gibson

Patrick Stewart

Conspiracy Theory is a sometimes funny, sometimes very dark thriller about a man who is clearly mentally disturbed, but who also may have information that is dangerous to some very powerful people. It references just about every conspiracy theory out there, but is built around its own.

The Plot
Jerry Fletcher drives a cab in New York City. He's obsessed with conspiracy theories and not particularly choosy about what they are. He spouts off a relentless torrent of them to his passengers, but he also appears to have some genuine issues. He blacks out at times, nearly killing a passenger at one point, and doesn't seem quite grounded in reality. This isn't a casual conspiracy theorist or someone who just likes listening to them for amusement, Jerry has problems and he believes wholeheartedly in most every conspiracy theory.

Jerry is obsessed with Alice Sutton, as well, a US attorney. He met Alice when he saved her from a mugger and has been showing up at her office regularly since. She feels sympathy for him and talks to him sometimes, allowing him to hold forth on his conspiracy theories to her.

Jerry's creepier side comes out when Alice is off of work. When she's at home, he watches her through the window with binoculars, going so far as to tune the radio to the same station as her and singing along to the song with her from afar.

Alice's father was murdered when she was younger, something about which she has been trying to learn more for many years.

Jerry sees government license plates on the street one day and determines that they're CIA. He pursues them to an office building and confirms that they are. They see him on security cameras and capture him.

Jerry is dragged off somewhere and wakes up tied to a wheel-chair. His eyes are taped open and he's given an injection of LSD and interrogated. He comes around enough to attack the doctor, breaking his nose, and gets out of the building. He goes to find Alice and collapses at her office.

At the hospital, Jerry is under arrest and handcuffed to a bed. Alice talks with him for a while. Jerry asks if she would swap out the chart on his bed with another bed, thinking someone's coming to get him. Alice refuses and leaves.

She returns the next day and one of the men in custody in the same room as Jerry has died of a heart attack. Jerry believes that Alice swapped the charts. The CIA and the FBI have both shown up, including the doctor who interrogated Jerry with the LSD.

Jerry fakes having a heart attack and manages to escape, part of the bed railing still handcuffed to his wrist. He is chased through the hospital but manages to get out.

The FBI seems more forthcoming with Alice. As she and an agent named Lowry look through Jerry's belongings, the CIA comes in and takes everything.

Jerry sneaks out of the hospital and hides in Alice's car, surprising her when she gets in. They go to Jerry's apartment. He places a beer bottle on the door knob so he can hear anyone trying to break in.

Jerry shows Alice around her apartment. He produces a conspiracy newsletter, has copious files and his apartment appears to be lined in tinfoil. He also has many copies of the book *Catcher in the Rye*. He tells Alice that he has to keep purchasing the book, but he doesn't know why. He's never even read the book, but has a bookshelf full of copies.

A SWAT team raids the house, but Jerry has an escape route built in. He and Alice get out through a hidden trapdoor. Jerry sets off charges in the house. It wasn't lined in tinfoil, but was built so that it could be completely incinerated without setting the rest of the building on fire. He uses the distraction to get out of the building, having planned every step ahead of time.

They get back to Alice's apartment. She finds out that Jerry's been stalking her and tells him to leave. At his apartment, Alice saw an image of herself on one of his collages, and he's clearly been obsessing over her without her knowledge.

Jerry knocks out one FBI agent and holds Lowry at gunpoint outside of Alice's house. He tells the agents not to harm her and disappears after knocking Lowry out.

He then purchases a copy of *Catcher in the Rye*. The transaction is immediately picked up by the CIA, letting them know Jerry's location.

Jerry again eludes the pursuing CIA squad and Alice finds out that everyone who subscribed to Jerry's newsletter, save for one, is dead. The agents come after Alice, but Jerry helps her escape.

Alice tracks down the only living subscriber to Jerry's newsletter. It turns out to be Dr. Jonas, the same CIA doctor who tortured and interrogated Jerry. He tells Alice how he worked for MKUltra and trained assassins for the CIA. Jerry is one of those assassins and he is actually the man who killed Alice's father, hence the obsession, according to Dr. Jonas.

Convinced, Alice agrees to help the CIA apprehend Jerry. She gets in touch with him and takes along a pizza box with a tracking device in it. Along the way, Jerry notices the car tailing him and causes an accident. He has a second car waiting nearby, gets in it and leaves, evading the pursuers.

Alice still believes he's crazy, so she calls her office and leaves the line open so that they can track her. Jerry heads back to Alice's family home and starts to recall what happened to him. He was, indeed, programmed as an assassin and was supposed to kill Alice's father. He couldn't do it, however, and told her father that he would protect Alice. Another assassin actually killed her father.

As Alice finds all this out, the CIA shows up in helicopters. The two make a run for it. The CIA gets Jerry and takes him off with them. Alice narrowly escapes being killed.

Alice finds out that Lowry is really not an FBI agent. He's

from a supervisory intelligence agency and is after Dr. Jonas. Jerry gets tortured some more. Alice realizes that a picture she saw at Jerry's house is connected and finds that the building in the picture is visible from a mental institution. She goes in and finds Jerry with the help of a guard.

The CIA is there, however, and they catch up to Jerry and Alice before they can escape. Lowry shows up, however, and a fight breaks out. Jerry tries to kill Jonas but Alice ends up shooting him.

Jerry is carted off in an ambulance and the film picks up later on. Alice has his union pin from being a cab driver. As she's riding her horse, Lowry, a man who had posed as a homeless friend to Jerry and Jerry himself are driving alongside her. Jerry cannot let anyone know he's alive because of the investigation, but he leaves Alice a sign that he survived, which she finds at the end of the film.

Appreciation for the True Paranoids
This film has some very dark parts to it and some very light-hearted ones. Among the best moments in the film, however, are those where Jerry is riding in his cab or talking to people casually. He's obsessed with his conspiracy theories and he knows them inside out. He believes so many different conspiracy theories that he seems utterly detached from reality.

Of course, Jerry is detached from reality, but not because he's simply delusional. He has, in fact, been manipulated by a shadowy government organization—the CIA, in this case—and had his memory fried out so much that he can't remember a thing about his former life at the outset of the film.

Jerry is very likeable, if weird. He's creepy with Alice and, if the film hadn't revealed his other history, the character would have even been somewhat scary. The film does a good job of allowing him to be genuinely creepy at times, making us wonder during the first act if he's really insane or not.

There are nice touches in this film that show some real love of conspiracy theories in general. Jerry explains what makes a good conspiracy theory; you can't prove it. His substitute for a logical process involves wandering through dates, names, imagined connections between events and tying them all together in some vast narrative that's really not at all believable, but one can see how Jerry got there.

Jerry is part of the conspiracy theory subculture, but he's not just musing, which is what makes this film interesting. Some of what Jerry believes is likely true and it's reasonable, at the end of the film, to suspect that he knows a lot of secrets. It's harder to believe, however, that someone like Dr. Jonas wouldn't simply have killed him rather than risk having him wandering around telling someone the truth.

The film references so many different conspiracies that it's hard to keep up. The most important one to this film is the MKUltra program, however. Unlike many other conspiracy theories—and apparently making it a bad one, at least in Jerry's estimation—MKUltra is well documented and very real.

MKUltra

From the 1950s until the 1960s, the CIA conducted experiments in mind control on unknowing human test subjects. Those experiments used US and Canadian citizens. The experiments included the use of drugs on unsuspecting test subjects, as well as techniques that used sensory deprivation, sexual abuse, verbal abuse and more.

The link above leads to Princeton University's page on this experiment. This was very real and is not a conspiracy theory in any regard.

In the film, Jerry's ordeal is connected to this. Dr. Jonas obviously still has an affinity for using psychedelics for mind control purposes in this film. Whatever he did to Jerry clearly destroyed a part of him. Jerry might actually be telling the truth about Dr. Jonas, but he's clearly paranoid as well.

This film uses the MKUltra program for the plot, but doesn't get too dark about it. The film shows how it affected Jerry, but doesn't really get into it much more than that. The film is still enjoyable, however.

Enjoying this Paranoid Thriller

Mel Gibson has become a controversial figure recently, but he's really quite good in this film. He's funny, likeable and Jerry is an interesting character. The film manages to show someone who is about as over-the-top conspiracy theorists get, but doesn't at all get condescending about it. Jerry is maintained as someone to sympathize with and root for, not laugh at.

That being said, the film really does have fun with conspiracy theories in general. Jerry raps them off so quickly that it's almost impossible to keep up with him. He tells them in a way that is so sincere and credulous that none of it is offensive or sinister. He just believes some strange things about the world, has a propensity for finding connections between things that are likely not at all related and comes up with some great stories in the process.

Alice is a bit thin as a character, really only existing to help us understand Jerry, but she's good for the role and she gives the viewers someone relatable to follow. The CIA certainly isn't relatable in this film. They're outright villains or, at least, Dr. Jonas and his crew are villains within the agency. Whatever organization Lowry works for is an interesting concept. They're apparently charged with keeping an eye on the most convert organizations out there but are even more unaccountable and secretive. It's an interesting premise, as it's exactly the kind of agency that someone like Jerry would likely suspect of being behind every bad event that ever happened, but they turn out to be the only good guys.

Patrick Stewart is great as Dr. Jonas. For a role like this, the actor has to be serious and sinister, but also likeable. When he's talking to Alice, he comes across as very sincere and like someone who's really just trying to stop a dangerous man who has gone completely out of control. He's still sinister, but he comes across as being sinister for the right reasons. When he's interrogating Jerry, however, Dr. Jonas is downright scary.

This film has a lot of comedy and action in it, so the thriller element is not nearly as intense as it is in other films. Any viewer who has seen action films knows that Jerry and Alice aren't going to get killed, so the tension is somewhat diminished, but *Conspiracy Theory* is still worth seeing. It has fun with paranoia, but doesn't for a moment pretend that all paranoia is unfounded, even among the most out-there conspiracy theorists.

The Insider (1999)

Director:

Michael Mann

Starring:

Al Pacino

Christopher Plummer

Diane Venora

Russell Crowe

The Insider tells the story of Dr. Jeffrey Wigand, a former Brown and Williamson Tobacco Company director of research and development and biochemist who blew the whistle on tobacco company disinformation and cover-ups in the 1990s. The film is critically acclaimed and provides some very intense, paranoia-inducing scenes based on real life events.

The Plot
The Insider is well over 2 hours long and the plot is very complex, involving several different stories that all mesh into the larger narrative.

The outset of the film takes place in Beirut, Lebanon, where we're introduced to Lowell Bergman, a producer for 60 Minutes. He sets up an interview with the founder of Hezbollah, being driven to a secret location, blindfolded and having to convince the sheikh to consent to be interviewed without being privy to the questions beforehand and while the sheikh is under the impression that the American media is "pro-Zionist" and ultimately biased against him. Lowell manages to set up the interview, with Mike Wallace coming in to do the actual on-camera question and answer.

We're then introduced to Dr. Jeffrey Wigand. In his first on-screen appearances, he's clearly discouraged, surly and holding something back. Finally questioned by his wife, Liane, he admits that he's been fired from his job at Brown and Williamson. He's been given a severance package and retains his medical benefits; important as his daughter suffers from severe asthma.

When Lowell gets back to California from the Middle East, he receives an anonymous package. He finds it full of internal tobacco company documents form Philip Morris. The documents have to do with the ignition characteristics of tobacco. Unable to decipher what they say for himself, he gets a friend at the FDA to set him up with someone who can understand the technical jargon in the documents.

The friend recommends Wigand, but Wigand initially wants nothing to do with Lowell. Wigand is under a confidentially agreement, breaking which would mean losing his severance package from Brown and Williamson. Eventually, Lowell persuades Wigand to meet him at a hotel.

Wigand agrees to give an interpretation of the documents for around $10,000. However, he strongly emphasizes to Lowell that he cannot say anything else about his work for tobacco companies. Lowell locks on to the fact that Wigand is intimidated by something and gets more curious.

Shortly afterward, Sandefur, the CEO of Brown and Williamson, calls Wigand in for a meeting. He makes some allusions to Wigand's family, angering Wigand, and then demands that Wigand sign a more restrictive confidentiality agreement. Wigand is enraged, believing that Lowell gave him up and potentially cost him his benefits and pay.

Lowell shows up at Wigand's house and confronts him face to face. Offended that Wigand is implying that he broke his word, Lowell explains that his entire career is based on keeping his word and that he's never burned a source. Wigand realizes that Lowell didn't give him up and, in Wigand's car, Wigand talks about those he calls the Seven Dwarfs, the seven tobacco company CEOs who testified before Congress that they did not believe that nicotine was addictive. According to Wigand, those statements were outright perjury and the CEOs knew better.

Lowell knows that he's sitting on a big story and starts working out ways that the crew at 60 Minutes can get Wigand to come forward. Because Wigand is under a confidentiality agreement and B&W has leverage over him, he's hesitant. They come up with an idea. If Wigand were to give testimony in one of the lawsuits against the tobacco companies, his testimony would be on the public record and therefore safe to use. Being compelled to testify would also allow Wigand to get around his confidentiality agreement. Once the testimony was public record, Wigand could speak to 60 Minutes on camera.

Wigand gets a job as a teacher. His background in chemistry and his fluency in Japanese help him to get hired, but the pay is much lower than he got with the tobacco companies and his family moves into a middle-class home. Wigand starts to find evidence that he's being watched.

Lowell starts preparing Wigand for what he's facing. He presses him about his background, trying to find out any information that could be dredged up and used for character assassination by the tobacco companies. Wigand mentions a few incidents, but nothing particularly serious.

The attorney general of Mississippi has filed a lawsuit against the tobacco companies to get reimbursement for Medicaid expenses. Lowell contacts the attorneys involved in the case and asks them about having Wigand testify. The attorneys are very interested in the idea.

Wigand begins to receive emailed death threats. He also finds a bullet in his mailbox. Lowell tells him to call the FBI. When the FBI agents show up, they act in an accusatory manner toward Wigand and seize his computer. Lowell immediately contacts a friend at the FBI, who initially complains that he has too much to do to bother looking at the agents' behavior anytime soon. Lowell brings up a string of connections between former and current FBI agents and the tobacco company. Motivated by the fear of embarrassing publicity, the FBI agent agrees to look into what happened.

Wigand shows up and does his interview in NYC. He brings to light a host of facts that expose the lies behind years of tobacco company claims.

The tobacco companies not only know that nicotine is addicting, they also consider themselves to be in the business of delivering nicotine to their customers. They manipulate the tobacco using ammonia chemistry to make the nicotine hit harder. He goes so far as to accuse the Seven Dwarves of lying before Congress.

Wigand's marriage starts to fall apart. Lowell, recognizing that there are increasing threats to Wigand's safety, leans on a friend at a security firm and gets Wigand's family a professional security detail.

Wigand heads to Mississippi to give his testimony, but is served with a restraining order on the way. The restraining order is valid in the state of Kentucky, but a Louisiana judge has refused to honor it. It was made at the request of B&W. Aware that he could go to jail for offering his testimony, at least if he goes back to Kentucky, Wigand eventually decides to go ahead and go on the record.

When Wigand gets to Kentucky, he finds out that his wife has filed for a divorce.

60 Minutes is initially ready to run with their story, but a lawyer for CBS corporate comes in and tells them about a legal practice called tortious interference. The idea is that CBS could be sued by B&W for damages over their causing Wigand to break his confidentiality agreement. The worse the information leaked, the higher the damage and, therefore, the more that CBS could be sued for.

CBS caves, with the president of CBS News, Erick Kluster, wanting to edit the interview to avoid liability. Mike Wallace goes along with this, and Lowell is not only against it, but offended by what he sees as spinelessness on the part of the network. He mentions that the liability issue might affect the financial interests of those involved in the proposed buyout of CBS. The lawyer who brought up the liability issue has millions riding on the sale.

B&W investigates Wigand and tries to release damaging information about him. The *Wall Street Journal* bites, but Lowell gets them to hold off on publishing the information before he can verify that it's all true. Lowell calls on another friend, a PI and attorney, to look into the allegations in B&Ws report.

Lowell gets sent on a forced vacation and 60 Minutes airs the Wigand piece in its abridged form. Wigand is enraged and Lowell, again, has to assure Wigand that he had nothing to do with manipulating Wigand and that he didn't give his blessing to the abridged interview.

The WSJ publishes an article about the B&W investigation into Wigand, calling it character assassination and pointing out lies and misrepresentations in the report found by Lowell's investigator. They also publish the contents of Wigand's testimony in Mississippi in the same issue.

60 Minutes airs the full interview, but after the story has already been broken. Lowell quits over the damage done to his reputation and his distaste for the behavior of CBS.

Wigand went on to be a successful teacher and the tobacco companies ended up paying out over 200 billion dollars in damages over their dangerous products. Lowell went on to work for Frontline, on PBS, and to become a professor of Journalism at UC Berkeley.

Real Paranoia and Intimidation

Where paranoia is concerned, *The Insider* outdoes many movies in this genre. To begin with, this is based on a real story, so the intimidation tactics are done in a real world setting. That means that they're subtle, but very effective. Wigand is an excellent golfer and one night, while relaxing at a driving range, a goon shows up at a nearby tee and stares at Wigand. The goon then follows him to his car and, from his own car, continues to stare at him. When Wigand gets out and yells at the man to stay away from him, the man pulls away before Wigand can do anything about it.

It gets worse, with the nighttime visits and the allegations that the B&W investigators dig up or fabricate out of whole cloth to discredit Wigand. By the time they drop the bullet off in the mailbox, the goons have pushed Wigand to the edge.

As is mentioned in the title cards at the end of the film, it was never established who was actually trying to intimidate Wigand. It doesn't take Poirot to figure out who would have had the motive, the means and the opportunity, however.

Wigand goes through hell, simply to tell the truth. This truth isn't about a government conspiracy or a political conspiracy, however. It's about a corporate conspiracy to hide health information from consumers to increase corporate profits. It's a familiar story to anyone who follows the news—or who likes these types of movies, for that matter—and one that is all too frightening in its implications. When the FBI agents show up and seem to be working for someone other than the FBI, the effect is downright frightening and maddening.

Not Being Intimidated

Lowell is one of the most engaging characters in this film. He has many of the same resources at his disposal that the people intimidating Wigand have. With a few phone calls, he can get investigators to verify or invalidate information, he can intimidate government officials into doing their job by letting them know what information he has and, when things get bad, he even comes through with some very intimidating security guards for Wigand and his family. He's one of the few characters in these types of films that are basically impossible to intimidate. He doesn't back down, doesn't break his word and takes care of the people who rely on his ethics and courage.

Mike Wallace is not portrayed particularly well in this film. CBS defended him. Wallace also changed his mind on his initial support to take out the most damaging parts of Wigand's interview. There is controversy about his portrayal in the film and, by other accounts, he did back agree to allowing them to air the full interview He felt let down by the network. While Wallace may not come off as committed to truth telling no matter what the risks for Lowell in this film, he also comes off as someone who does not take well to intimidation. The scene where he finally has enough of the CBS attorney calling him "Mike", rather than Mr. Wallace, is particularly gratifying.

Enjoying this Paranoid Thriller

There is no reason why people who are fans of this genre shouldn't enjoy this film. *The Insider* is based on real life incidents and one of the biggest corporate conspiracies ever unearthed. The film has a very long run time but at no point does it feel as though it is dragging its feet.

The performances in this film are stellar. Pacino, Plumber and Crowe all bring a great deal of intensity and authenticity to their roles. Crowe's Wigand is an extraordinary man, but he's also very regular in many regards. In the scenes where we see him teaching, we see what really inspires him. This is a man who really does love science. By his own admission, he took the tobacco company work because of the money, but you can see the agony in him resulting from what he knows. A scientist, he doesn't like bad information. He watches his own children suffer with asthma, gasping for breath the same way many smokers do at the end of their artificially shortened lives. He might have worked for a very dirty business, but he's a good man at heart, and it makes him something of an everyday hero.

Lowell's character helps the audience to navigate the intricacies of what's going on. Early in the film, we see his office, plastered with a Caesar Chavez poster and other activist memorabilia, showing that he has the heart of someone who feels he represents something bigger than himself. The way that Pacino portrays him never loses sight of that essential truth about the man. He can handle dealing with corporate thugs, litigious lawyers and others who roadblock the truth, but he loses it when someone questions his integrity. The most important thing to this man seems to be that people know he isn't like the people he reports about. He doesn't burn anyone and his actions during Wigand's ordeal prove that over and over again.

You can watch the Wigand interview on line at CBS. It's historically significant, of course, and knowing a bit about what went into making it happen makes it even more powerful. While the film gives a great deal of background on what happened, seeing Mike Wallace run down the list of actions taken against Wigand to try to get him to keep quiet makes it even more powerful. Wallace also reveals the problems with the threatened litigation and CBS shutting down the full interview.

The Insider is a great film. It has everything that makes a great story work. The main characters are engaging, the drama feels real—because it is real—and the stakes are genuinely high at every point in the story.

"We're in the nicotine delivery business." This simple truth that was known, but denied publically, by the tobacco industry is stated early in the actual interview. It dismantled the no-one-knows defense used by tobacco companies to avoid billions in potential liability. It's still powerful to hear Wigand say it so many years after it aired.

Like *All the President's Men* and other films of such high caliber, this one is based in real life and is all the more engaging because of that. *The Insider* is most certainly worth watching for any fan of quality filmmaking.

Enemy of the State (2005)

Director:

Tony Scott

Starring:

Gene Hackman

John Voight

Will Smith

Enemy of the State is an oddly prescient film from the late 1990s. It follows a lawyer as he is inadvertently caught up in a government conspiracy to make it easier to spy on Americans, a conspiracy backed by some very murderous and unaccountable people with tremendous technology at their disposal.

The Plot
In the opening of the film, we meet an ethical US congressman named Hamersley as he discusses a new piece of legislation with a high ranking NSA official, Reynolds. Hamersley opposes a new piece of legislation that the NSA wants, which will make it much easier for the NSA to spy on the activities of everyday Americans.

The conversation goes sour and, while the congressman is walking back to his car, he is attacked by NSA thugs, who inject him with something, push his car into the lake and make it look like the congressman had a fatal accident. The NSA agents don't know it, but a wildlife research camera is located across the lake, operated by Daniel Zavitz, and has caught all of the action, and the killers' faces, on tape.

Robert Clayton Dean is a labor lawyer trying to help out working people. He's recently been involved in a case where a mob boss has been intimidating workers to vote in a way that favors the mob. Dean confronts the mobsters, showing their leader a video that shows the mob boss, who is legally barred from having contact with labor organizations, fraternizing with a union boss. He threatens to send the video to the authorities, provoking a confrontation. The mob boss agrees to leave the workers alone, but wants to know who made the video. On the way out, Dean is made aware that the FBI is watching the restaurant where the mobsters operate.

The NSA isn't long in finding out that there's a video of the incident. They dispatch two disgraced ex-Marines to get Zavitz. Zavitz realizes that they're coming and puts the footage on a digital drive and hides it in a hand-held video game. As he flees, he runs through a lingerie store where Dean is buying his girlfriend a present. Zavitz manages to stuff the video game in Dean's bag undetected and flees. He runs outside and gets run over by a fire truck. A conspiracy theorist and journalist who is alerted to the existence of the tape by Zavitz is also killed by the NSA goons.

The NSA realizes that Dean likely has the video and bugs his house. They then start destroying his reputation. They set up a phony affair between Dean and a colleague that nearly destroys Dean's marriage. He ends up losing his job, having his credit accounts cancelled, and having his bank accounts seized.

Desperate, Dean manages to call on one of his resources, Rachel Banks, the woman with whom he is accused of having an affair but who also provides him with information and contacts for his cases when needed. She sets him up with a man named Brill.

The NSA sends in someone to pose as Brill, but the real Brill shows up and helps Dean out. He informs Dean that his clothes are probably full of tracking devices and that Brill needs to get away. Brill escapes. Dean gets chased by the NSA heavies through a hotel, finally having to shed all of this clothing to avoid being tracked.

The NSA gets to Banks and kills her. They then frame Dean for the congressman's murder. With Brill's help, whose real name is Lyle, Dean finally realizes why the NSA is after him when Brill gets to the footage on the storage card. Soon after they do, however, the NSA shows up and leads them on a chase. The evidence gets destroyed, apparently leaving Dean framed for the murder and his life torn apart.

Dean, however, isn't having it and wants to fight back. Brill reveals his past. He was formerly with the NSA, a communications expert. He managed to get out of Iran before the revolution, but his partner was killed. He has been hiding out ever since and encourages Dean to do the same. Dean decides to go after the NSA.

Brill suggests using the NSA's own tactics against them. He first gets footage of a congressman who supports the surveillance bill having an affair and uses it to blackmail him. He then bugs the congressman's room, using the same bugs that the NSA used. To further the frame up, he starts making deposits into Reynolds's bank accounts, giving the appearance that Reynolds is accepting bribes.

With everyone set up, Brill and Dean meet with Reynolds. Brill tells Dean that he can capture footage of the meeting for 2 minutes, but that he has to flee the scene as soon as that mark has passed. Brill manages to get Reynolds on tape, admitting too much of the plot, but Dean waits too long and the NSA goons catch him and Brill.

Interrogated at gun point, Dean tells Reynolds that the same mobsters from the beginning of the film have the video of the congressman's murder. The NSA goes to the restaurant where the mobsters meet, dragging Dean along with them. Dean tricks the mobsters into thinking that Reynolds has the footage that the mob boss wants, with the NSA believing that the mobsters have the footage that Reynolds wants. A gunfight ensues, with the mobsters and the NSA agents and thugs all shooting each other, save for one old mobster in the restaurant kitchen.

In the end, Dean is cleared of the murder and the plot is revealed. Dean flips channels on his television and sees himself. He realizes that Brill has bugged his apartment as a prank. Brill then transmits a video of himself and his cat on a tropical beach as a farewell to Dean.

Not as Dark as Others, but Possibly More Accurate
There are some very dark, paranoid thrillers in this book. *The Parallax View, Marathon Man, JFK, Syriana* and many of the others in this book are very menacing films built on very disturbing stories. This film is a bit lighter than the aforementioned. The escaping protagonists even manage to save Brill's cat from harm and Will Smith has some very funny moments in this film, as does Hackman as the surly ex-NSA agent. While it certainly seems unintentional, this film did end up predicting some of what would happen in the future.

Edward Snowden, a former NSA contractor, leaked information in 2013 that revealed a vast NSA spying program that was largely directed at American citizens. The spying program he revealed was not unlike the one Reynolds is gunning for in this film. The NSA is shown as being able to track locations, phone calls, computer records, bank statements and other information on anyone located most anywhere in the world. This spying program included collusion with tech companies, the collection of phone records without warrants and beyond. For those who believed in the global security state and its vast overreach, the revelation was akin to Lee Harvey Oswald rising from the grave and letting JFK conspiracy theorists know for sure that he was a patsy. It was every worst nightmare of the paranoid realized, and the controversy continues today.

Enemy of the State, though it might have seemed far-fetched and just a good paranoid thriller when it was released, has proven to have been predictive. The world that Dean and Brill are fighting against is the world that we live in today. Phones are tapped, calls are monitored, locations are recorded, emails are read, Internet traffic is monitored and more. This has all moved from the realm of conspiracy theory to that of government policy, with unaccountable agencies that are charged with some of the most powerful technology in existence being busted lying to Congress about their activities. Just like Reynolds in *Enemy of the State*, this is all done under the justification of national security. The series of cover-ups and falsehoods that comes in response to questions about all of this surveillance seems to have been going on for some time as well.

Enemy of the State manages to mix a dark story up with some great action sequences and one of the most charismatic actors working right now. It also, however, predicted with near complete accuracy the reality of what was to come in the years and decades ahead. With that in mind, it's hard to see this film as a movie and rate it on its own merits, since it does hit so very close to home.

Enjoying this Paranoid Thriller

The rather shocking accuracy of this film aside, it also happens to have a great star as the lead and an excellent story. It keeps the tension high throughout and Smith is great as a rather fish-out-of-water character. He proves himself intelligent and resourceful, making him even more likeable, as he learns to evade his pursuers and learns a bit about spy craft itself from Brill.

The film doesn't shy away from being funny at times, which gives the audience something of a break from the rather violent action that goes on. It opens with a murder and the mob boss certainly seems like a serious guy, but Dean manages to be funny and engaging and entirely relatable. What we know about him at the outset is that he's a good lawyer and that he cares about his clients. He like nailing the bad guys when he can, and doesn't mind confronting them face to face to protect a client, showing he has some real backbone beneath all that charm.

Brill provides the necessary information dump for Dean when he reveals the plot, how the NSA works and so forth. There's enough of a conspiracy here, and it's fleshed out enough, to keep the film interesting.

One of the most interesting characters is the NSA tech played by Jack Black. He's the new breed of spy. He's not a cold-blooded killer like James Bond who can shoot straight, kill with his bare hands and outwit and outclass the bad guys at every turn. He's an overweight, cocky hacker who uses computers to track down enemies of the NSA and who unquestioningly takes orders from his corrupt bosses.

Good performances, a good plot and very well-shot action sequences all make this a film worth seeing. It's eerily predictive story makes it even more so.

Mercury Rising (1998)

Director:

Harold Becker

Starring:

Alec Baldwin

Bruce Willis

Chi McBride

Miko Hughes

Mercury Rising doesn't break any new ground in the paranoid thriller genre, but it does provide some good action sequences and an interesting plot. The film centers on Art Jeffries and Simon Lynch as they try to keep ahead of murderous government agents.

The Plot
At the opening of the film, Art Jeffries, an undercover FBI agent, is in the midst of a bank robbery gone wrong. He's infiltrated a militia and the leader of the organization, Edgar, is determined to have a shootout with the FBI, who wants to negotiate.

Art tries to let the FBI knows that he needs more time and that he can bring everyone out of the situation alive, but the FBI moves in under the direction of an agent named Hartley. The militia members, including the leader's teenage son, get killed in the firefight that ensues.

Art punches out Hartley and gets reprimanded in Washington. He maintains that he was in the right and that Hartley did not have to go in shooting. Nonetheless, Art is assessed as suffering from paranoia and assigned to rookie duties, such as monitoring wiretaps.

Meanwhile, a young, autistic boy named Simon, who lives with his mother and father in Chicago, shows an incredible facility for figuring out puzzles. While reading a world-hunt puzzle in a magazine, he deciphers a hidden message. It's a phone number, which he calls. The phone number rings the NSA, whose agents put the puzzle in the magazine.

The puzzle was planted to take the "geek factor" into consideration. The puzzle was written in a code named "Mercury". Lt. Colonel Nick Kudrow, of the NSA, has a lot riding on this code, which was believed to be unbreakable. He orders the death of the boy and his parents, setting it up as a murder/suicide.

The assassins visit Simon's house and kill his parents. Simon, hearing the police sirens, hides in a crawlspace. Art is sent in to investigate the murder/suicide, but he quickly figures out that it's some sort of a setup. He finds Simon and, despite not knowing how to handle him at first, helps get him to a hospital.

Burrell, an NSA killer, goes after Simon at the hospital. Art intercepts him, however, and manages to get Simon out. He makes it to the train but another agent follows him and the boy. Art ambushes the killer on the train and kills him.

The NSA starts putting out information that Art kidnapped Simon. Art goes to the house of another special agent, Tommy, to seek refuge. Tommy and his family help out with Simon and Tommy lets Art take his car, agreeing not to report it stolen until the morning.

Art falls asleep in the car and Simon wanders off. Simon gives directions back to his house. The police show up after Art gets to further investigate what went on.

The NSA agents who were maintaining the phone line don't want the child assassinated, so they find ways to work around Kudrow. One of them agrees to meet with Art; using an FBI email account and the Mercury code, which the agent knows that Simon can decipher, he sets up the meeting. Art meets a girl named Stacy at the coffee shop. He cons her into watching Simon so he can meet with the agent.

Art meets the agent on the street and gets some information on what's going on. Shortly into their conversation, however, the agent is killed when Burrell shoots him. Burrell and Art have a chase through the Chicago streets; Burrell loses him.

Simon takes a liking to Stacey. Art returns and picks up Simon but, later that night, they both go to Stacey's. Art needs a place to stash Simon where he'll be safe. Stacy cancels a business trip to help Art and Simon out.

The other NSA agent, Pedranski, gets a typewriter so he can write higher-ups about Kudrow's corruption. The NSA kills him before he can send the letter, however. His girlfriend manages to get the carbon paper from the letter to Art. Pedranski didn't get to sign his letter, but his fingerprints are on the carbon paper.

Art goes after Kudrow. He goes to his house, meeting the Lt.

Col in his wine cellar. The two argue and Kudrow starts giving a speech about patriotism and protecting intelligence assets. Art kicks him in the sternum and walks out, leaving Kudrow on the floor.

Stacey called Tommy and Tommy managed to set her and Simon up with witness protection. Kudrow intervenes at the FBI and tries to get Tommy in trouble for setting up witness protection for false reasons.

Tommy's superior agrees to let Kudrow take care of the witness protection, but Tommy shows him the fingerprints on the carbon paper and gives him other information. The FBI supervisor realizes that Kudrow is trying to kill Simon and sends out an FBI assault team to the meeting place.

The FBI assault team manages to stop Kudrow and Burrell. Burrell gets killed while shooting it out with the FBI. Kudrow fights Art on the ledge of the building. Simon gets Kudrow's gun, which he had dropped, and gives it to Art. Art shoots Kudrow and Kudrow plunges from the building.

At the end of the film, Art goes to visit Simon. Although he didn't expect him to, Simon remembers Art and hugs him.

A Good Example of the Formula
Mercury Rising is not an innovative film. It follows several different conventions but, for people who are looking for this type of film, it delivers.

It's an action film first and foremost, with the action sequences being motivated by a basic conspiracy plot. The source of all the trouble in this film, the Mercury code, is entirely fictional. It's entirely possible to make an unbreakable code. In addition to the enigmatic historical examples linked, a Vernam cipher, also called a one-time pad, is unbreakable and simple. In fact, that type of code is so secure that the encoded messages are broadcast over short wave radio numbers stations, which anyone with a short wave radio receiver can listen to.

In short, the Mercury cipher wouldn't really have been worth killing anyone over, much less a young, autistic child who posed no real threat to anyone.

Nonetheless, Kudrow is fully willing to kill over it. The film starts out with the reengage cop formula. Art is a great cop who knows how to do his job but who is foiled by incompetent superiors. He gets busted down in duty because of his attitude, but mostly because he happens to be right.

When the NSA assassinates Simon's parents, the film takes on the paranoid thriller structure. Kudrow and Burrell are the big bads. The NSA, however, is not depicted as entirely evil. Two of the biggest sources of help that Art has come from the NSA, once Kudrow's brutal methods turn them against the organization.

Simon is the precious cargo, of course, and the film actually does use his autism well to make the situation tenser. Instead of being given heroic rescue after heroic rescue, Art has to shelter Simon as best he can. It's just impossible to protect Simon any other way. Simon gets horribly distressed by any kind of violent stimulation and is uncontrollable. In the end, however, he comes through for Art and saves his life, in fact.

The investigation arc here is short and to the point. Once Art understands that Simon deciphered the code and that's why Kudrow wants him dead, there's really nothing left to investigate. For audiences that like pulling back the layers of a vast conspiracy with the protagonist, this might be a bit disappointing. For audiences that want more action, however, the exploration of the conspiracy will likely be plenty. It's enough to establish Kudrow as a very bad guy who has access to all kinds of advanced technology to follow Simon and Art.

Stacey is the basic captive female helper that appears in some of these films. She gets fooled into helping Art and Simon, rather than coerced, but she not only risks herself to help them when she finds out, but seems to genuinely want to help as well. Her character doesn't have much to do, really, other than be there with Simon in some scenes, but, again, the character serves the purposes of the structure and is well played.

The ending fight is predictable, but Baldwin is nasty enough as Kudrow to make his fate satisfying.

Beyond the formula, there are some more interesting elements here, however.

The Blue Collar Dad

Bruce Willis, despite being one of the most well-known actors around, has a lot of regular-person charisma. He plays that up here and, even though *Mercury Rising* is very formulaic, it doesn't treat the audience like idiots. Simon's dad is a working-class guy. He's a big, burly man who works long hours but who's very caring and kind to Simon. It sets up Simon so that the idea of him bonding with another hard-working, big burly guy who's also likeable—Willis—is believable enough.

The bad guys in this film are all managerial types. Kudrow is set up as someone who bosses people around and stabs them in the back to get ahead when he has to, or probably even when he just feels like stabbing someone in the back. Kudrow is effective, but one gets the idea that his position isn't one he earned by being good at his job, but one he earned by doing whatever it took to keep everyone else around him down.

Kudrow has the advantage of the most advanced technology, networks of information and hitmen to back up his plans. Art has to get by with what he has, rely on people to help him out now and then, and doesn't seem to understand technology very well at all.

There's a bit of outsider romanticizing on display here. The film doesn't imply that everything that's going on is the work of a huge conspiracy, and it tends to give the impression that it's really mostly Kudrow who's doing this. The FBI goes right after him when they find out that he is trying to kill Simon. In other conspiracy films, the FBI might have actually ended up helping Kudrow, being sucked into the conspiracy themselves.

Art, the good FBI agent that the system hates, is the only one who can stand up to Kudrow. Kudrow really has all the advantages where experience, intelligence and resources are concerned, so Art is an effective underdog here. Combine that with the fact that Bruce Willis is very good at making over-the-top heroes come off as average guys, and there is some fun to be had in this film. Watching Kudrow get unceremoniously kicked in the chest is particularly gratifying.

Enjoying this Paranoid Thriller
Mercury Rising is not like *Marathon Man*, *The Boys from Brazil*, *Three Days of the Condor* or other such heady fare. This film is all about the action. It's about watching Art save an autistic boy from brutal government assassins. In that regard, there are some things that make this film work.

The action sequences are over the top, but they fit this type of movie. This is the type of movie where, in order to be stealthy, an assassin disguises himself as a doctor and sneaks into a protected room in a hospital. He's obviously trying to go undetected. Under his smock, however, he's carrying an enormous handgun with an enormous silencer on it. In a building full of ways to kill people without being detected—pillows, even— he's going to depend on a silencer to quiet the round from his handgun enough to slip away.

This film, as was said, is not intellectual. It's not meant to be. It's more about the chase.

Simon presents a different kind of challenge than the protagonists usually have in these films. He's written as a character with a genuine disability, which is actually refreshing. In some films, problems that a protagonist or secondary character has will just disappear after a while. With Simon that doesn't happen. There is no way that Art can keep him alive in any other way than to keep him hidden. Simon is not capable of handling stress and overstimulation. Since the film keeps that going, it makes it interesting as far as the dynamic between the two characters.

It also implies that Simon and Art have some things in common. They both see things differently than others do. They also both see solutions. In the beginning of the film, Art is dealing with how to get the militia members to surrender. He basically cracks the code to this, such as it is. He figures out that he can turn the father against his son, not to kill the father, but to make him doubt. He just needs time, but the FBI agents around him don't see that and kill people who never had to die. Simon sees the code in the puzzle and, further, can solve it. Art makes an allusion to this in one scene.

This is really further along the action spectrum than it is the intellectual spectrum. It's definitely a thriller, definitely paranoid, but it's not a film about layers of conspiracy. It's a decent watch, however, definitely has its moments and Willis is excellent in these types of roles. In this case, he's a bit better than the script, which makes it fun enough to watch.

Interview with the Assassin (2002)

Director:

Neil Burger

Starring:

Dylan Haggerty

Raymond J. Barry

Interview with the Assassin is a mockumentary film that follows a down-on-his-luck cameraman who seems to get the story of a lifetime. Whether or not he did is left an open question, but this film does a good job of building tension and following one of the most popular conspiracy theories of all, the alleged conspiracy surrounding the JFK assassination.

The Plot

Ron Kobeleski is out of work as a cameraman. Having few prospects, he runs into his neighbor, Walter, who claims to have a huge story for him. Walter is dying of cancer and, reckoning that he has nothing to lose, decides to come forward with a huge revelation: He shot JFK.

Walter claims to have proof and, to begin establishing his story, he takes Ron to a safe deposit box where he has the casing from a spent rife round stored in a baggie. He says that this is the casing from the round used to shoot JFK and that he was the infamous second gunman of conspiracy theories, shooting from the equally infamous grassy knoll.

Ron takes the casing to be tested at a forensics lab. The casing comes back as having been shot somewhere around the time of the assassination. Ron asks if the technician could match it to the bullet if he had it. The technician says he could and then asks if it's the JFK round. Ron doesn't answer directly and the technician says he wouldn't touch it if it was, because it's too dangerous.

Walter and Ron go to Dallas. Walter walks around the scene of the assassination and shows him where he stood and so forth. He was the man on the grassy knoll.

Walter brings Ron to meet one of his Marine friends. He wants to get in touch with his former CO, who can back up his story. At his friend's house, Water shows impressive marksmanship skills, going so far as to fire live rounds at Ron while he's downrange.

Walter gets a call when they get back home, telling him he needs to stop. Ron arranges to meet with Walter's ex-wife. She doesn't want to talk to him at first and, even after she does sit down for an interview, she's very cautious with information.

She tells Ron that Walter is known liar and a thief, even having done time in prison for theft. Her marriage to him was not happy. When she's told that Walter is dying of cancer she says she's sorry to hear it, but she sounds indifferent.

Walter starts to act more unstable. He attacks a policeman in Virginia, but the man's SUV was in the hotel parking lot where Walter and Ron were staying the night before, apparently spying on them, at least according to Walter. Ron has possibly seen people creeping around his house at night on security cameras that he installed. Ron also may have been shadowed at a library, but everything is kept vague. Walter may or may not have murdered at least two people.

Walter eventually sneaks a weapon—which is registered to Ron—into a presidential news conference. Ron yells that there's a gun, but doesn't identify Walter, allowing him to escape. The gun is found in a trashcan outside the hotel and Walter knows that it will be traced back to him.

Ron heads home, fearing for his life. Walter confronts him at his house, wanting the tapes, and Ron ends up shooting him. The final sequences show Ron in prison. A title card at the end of the film reveals that Ron never finished out his sentence.

The Second Gunman

Interview with the Assassin follows a popular conspiracy theory that there was more than one shooter that fired at Kennedy. Some of these theories also hold that the shot that actually killed Kennedy did not come from the book depository, as was discussed earlier. The story in this film is built on that particular set of theories, but the story is really about whether Walter is the second shooter or not.

Walter is a very good shot, even at an older age. He seems callous and nasty enough to have no moral issues with carrying out an assassination. He says he was given a job and he did it and maintains this view toward shooting the president most of the time.

There is evidence that Walter was a member of a covert operations unit but, as is the case with everything else about Walter, there's always something that makes it seem off. The friend he meets seems to be one of his former comrades but, then again, he could just be someone as unbalanced as Walter who goes along with Walter's delusions.

Walter discloses a great deal of information about how he shot the president and where he stood. He explains how he snuck the rifle in, what kind of rifle it was and so forth. It could be impressive, but there has been so much investigation into and speculation surrounding Kennedy's assassination that anyone could say what Walter is saying. There's really nothing special about his explanation of the assassination, but he could be revealing the truth out of all the speculation, and that's what keeps Ron interested.

The way the tension is set up in this film involves constant doubt.

The Ambiguous Chase
Quite a few conspiracy thrillers get a lot of mileage out of the protagonist being pursued by a shadowy organization. Trying to figure out who they represent, what they're trying to suppress and so forth is part of the fun of these movies.

Interview with the Assassin plays this up by not making it apparent whether the protagonists are being pursued at all. Ron sees someone who appears to be following him one day, but he's no espionage agent and being with Walter is clearly making him paranoid. Ron's wife sees what might be someone lurking at the edge of the surveillance camera footage from outside their house. Then again, it might not be someone lurking at all.

Walter gets shadier and shadier as the film goes on. It's never apparent whether he's on a rampage or if he's just one step ahead of the people trying to stop him from disclosing what he knows. He attacks a cop, might have killed an old ally, probably killed someone to get identification, among other things. He seems to become increasingly paranoid as the two travel to Washington.

In the end, Walter manages to get through security at a presidential event with a weapon. He does this, he says, to prove that he could, but it's never clear whether or not Walter may have shot the president to prove his point.

This film doesn't really answer any of its own questions. Real fans of JFK conspiracy theories, however, may like it or may hate it.

Enjoying this Paranoid Thriller

As was said, people who are really into JFK conspiracies may really love or really hate this movie.

On one level, the film definitely implies that there is something shady going on. It's very easy to watch this and to take from it that Ron got too close to a conspiracy and ended up paying dearly for it. This follows the same story pattern as found footage films and, indeed, while this is a mockumentary, some parts of this film are shot in a very found footage style.

The film uses Ron as our skeptical guide to the world of JFK conspiracies. He's introduced to Walter, who is a very intimidating, sinister person, really. In one scene, Walter meets one of Ron's children and it's beyond creepy. There's something about Walter that never seems quite right. He might be mentally ill, but he's not like the vast majority of people who suffer from a mental illness. He also seems to be a predator and, in fact, that's part of what gives him a touch of credibility.

The multiple gunmen theories are some of the most popular among JFK conspiracy theorists. These theories generally hold that the assassination was the work of high up people who employed real assassins to kill JFK and that Lee Harvey Oswald was just a patsy. Walter comes off as being someone who could potentially be a hired assassin. He's dark, menacing, apparently murderous, emotionless and flat and sleazy. He seems like he crawled out from under a rock and that the world would be better off with him back under it.

In other words, if you're a JFK conspiracy theorist, Walter probably fits the mold for a second gunman. Skilled but stupid, absent of a sense of morality and quick to kill, that's Walter.

Conspiracy theorists may hate it for an entirely other way that this film can be seen.

Ron gets very involved in a conspiracy theory. The man telling him that he's the actual assassin who tried to kill Kennedy is clearly disturbed. He shoots at Ron to prove a point. Neither Ron nor any other sane human being would leave Walter alone with a child. Walter's ex-wife can barely talk about the man and seems only too glad to be rid of him as she does. He's a known liar; he's a thief.

Walter's telling of the assassination is generic. Anyone who had read more than two Kennedy conspiracy websites could probably go to the site of the assassination and say something very similar, throwing in as many facts as Walter does along the way.

Ron wasn't being critical enough. He didn't consider what Walter was saying and got seduced by the idea of finding out something huge. He got so caught up in it that he followed a lunatic around on a mass murder spree and nearly got killed himself. When people take this stuff too far, in other words, the result is paranoia, jumping at shadows and getting involved with very bizarre and unbalanced people.

This film never really answers whether or not Walter was telling the truth, but it does do a good job of showing why many people find the theories compelling; people not at all like Walter. Ron, as was said, is the skeptical audience member, basically. He finds out about one of the main conspiracy theories surrounding the Kennedy assassination through Walter and doesn't know quite what to make of it. On one level, Walter seems legit; on another, Walter never seems quite legit enough, as is the case for his story surrounding the assassination and his role in it.

This film uses the mockumentary format and, like many films in this genre, it drags at times. The found-footage segments are particularly slow at times and the odd look of these sequences is sometimes distracting. Likewise, some of the scares that the film goes for based on the supposed surveillance are a bit thin and don't amount to much.

The most interesting thing about this film is that it combines the decades-old Kennedy assassination theories with the latest thing in movies, found footage. Its ending strays from that format quite a lot but it does offer an updated way of dramatizing these conspiracy theories.

The Constant Gardener (2005)

Director:

Fernando Meirelles

Starring:

Bill Nighy

Danny Huston

Hubert Koundé

John Sibi-Okumu

Rachel Weisz

Ralph Fiennes

The Constant Gardener follows a man investigating his wife's death in Africa. A diplomat, her husband discovers a drug testing program being carried out in Africa, which knowingly violates ethical and safety guidelines and which exploits a population who think they're getting needed medications.

The Plot
Justin Quayle is a low-level British diplomat. At the beginning of the film, we find out that his wife, Tessa, has been killed. She was apparently murdered. The man who authorities suspect of her murder also turns up dead. A good friend of Tessa, Bluhm, was a close friend of hers and a physician with whom

she worked.

Tessa was an activist. She initially met Justin when she started interrogating him about the invasion of Iraq at a press conference. Though she did her best to embarrass Justin, he instantly took a liking to her. In flashback sequences, we learn how they fell in love and eventually married.

Tessa, however, was trying to get close to Justin for a reason. She and Bluhm had been investigating the practices of a pharmaceutical company. The company was running drug trials in Africa and committing many ethical and safety violations in the process. This is the reason that she was killed.

Justin wants to know why Tessa was killed and who killed her. He finds the connection to the pharmaceutical company, which was testing a drug called Dypraxa on the population. The population, however, impoverished and uninformed of the dangers of the drug, proved easy subjects to try it out on.

Justin soon learns that there are connections to the scandal within his own agency. Tessa was already on to this fact and had found information that linked one of the High Commissioners to the drug company's scheme. Justin also uncovers information that implies that Tessa and Bluhm were having an affair, but finds other information that indicates that Bluhm was actually gay. More and more, things start pointing to a conspiracy to cover up a murder.

Justin finds out what Tessa was trying to do. Aware that the drug company was testing a dangerous product on the poor population, she wanted to expose the plot and make sure that the company fixed the problems with the drug before releasing it on the market. The company, wanting to preserve its profits, wanted Tessa silenced to make sure that they could release the drug before anyone else could put a similar product on the market. One of Justin's own colleges, Pellegrin, was behind the murder, wanting to cover up the report.

Justin continues his investigation. He's foiled at every turn, whether it's by corrupt African cops or corrupt British officials or corrupt businessmen. He's the outsider here, and he becomes more and more aware of it. Justin, however, is a very clever sort. He engineers false stories—Tessa's diary—and uses them to find connections between people and uncover the conspiracy.

Justin soon finds information linking KDH, a drug company, and Three Bees, which tests Dypraxa in Africa and also happens to manufacture a pesticide that Justin uses in his gardening.

Justin starts to realize that he's being watched more than ever. He's assaulted by two men in his hotel room and receives a death threat.

He continues on with his investigation nonetheless. He starts to uncover the connections between the British government, the drug companies and the testing program. Of course, it comes down to jobs and money. Woodrow, a colleague in the British government, provides the information dump, letting Justin know about the plot to kill Tessa and the links between the drug companies, governments and moneyed interests.

An ex-spy reveals that there is a contract out on Justin. He also reveals how corporate murder works. It's all a series of phone calls until one of the calls finally reaches a hitman who takes care of whatever problem the company needs to go away. The ex-spy encourages Justin to quit, but he's far past the point of quitting. He describes how Bluhm was brutally tortured and murdered and again warns Justin that he's in real danger. The ex-spy gives Justin a gun for protection, but regrets that Justin is going to press on with his investigation.

Justin heads to Loki to find a doctor named Lorbeer, who works at a clinic and who provided the information that Tessa used in her report. Lorbeer has since started actually trying to help the population, disposing of expired drugs that the pharma companies donate, but that are well beyond their expiration dates.

As Lorbeer gives Justin information, another tribe attacks the village on horseback. Lorbeer has a copy of the report Tessa was working with, and gives it to Justin.

The tribesmen attack the village and commit a massacre, gunning down the villagers and burning their homes. Justin and Lorbeer flee, nearly getting killed by the pursuing horsemen. They manage to get out on a cargo plane. Abuk, a young girl who helps Lorbeer, is left behind, likely to die along with the rest of her village. Lorbeer gives Justin a final piece of evidence he needs. Lorbeer confesses that he was the one who started the chain of phone calls that led to Tessa's death.

Justin asks the pilot to be dropped off where Tessa's body was found. He knows he's going to die, given all that he's found out.

A voiceover of Justin's funeral accompanies footage of Justin wandering around where Tessa died, alleging that he killed himself. A speaker following Pellegrin reads the letter that Justin and Tessa were killed over and discusses in detail how Justin was clearly murdered, and Tessa as well, and lists off the real culprits, Pellegrin, KDH and the other actors involved.

In a flashback, Justin is shown talking to Tessa where she died—he's hallucinating—as a group of armed thugs drive up in a pickup truck. He tells Tessa's he's home as the thugs get out of the truck and approach him from behind. He stands up, turns to face them and the film ends.

Uncommonly Powerful

The Constant Gardener is unlike many of the films featured in this book. Many of them concentrate on the process of uncovering plots launched by corrupt, and sometimes downright evil, individuals and organizations. This film concentrates its focus on the good people who get caught up in these plots and plans.

Tessa is a great character. She's inspired, ethical, motivated to change the things she finds wrong about the world and outstandingly competent at what she does. She finds a great match in Justin. Justin works for a much different sort of organization than does Tessa, but he's her equal in terms of her ethics.

Part of what makes this film hard to watch is that the viewer knows how it's going to turn out. Justin and Tessa are so likeable that it makes it difficult to watch the story unfold, as it can only go to one place.

This film really shows how corporate and government conspiracies work. As the old spy says, someone makes a phone call to someone who makes a phone call and so on and, eventually, some men are dispatched and someone dies. It's all easy enough to cover up, happening on a continent where law enforcement is almost universally corrupt and where people can just disappear and no one's the wiser. The scene where the village is raided drives this home. Justin and Tessa are both in a place where mass murder happens in broad daylight and where the only thing that those who might otherwise intervene can do is to flee for their lives.

It also drives home the point of why Africa is so rich in opportunities for exploitation; disposable drugs for disposable patients, as Dr. Lorbeer says with distain. No one here matters. Everyone is subject to disappearing. Even the UN pilots, who seem to be among the most solid people in the film, cannot save the villagers. They're only authorized to save aid workers. Wherever Justin wanders in this film, there is massive stratification among people. His higher ups are smug and self-important, sure that they'll never be held accountable for anything that they do. The population itself is disposable. They're too poor to cause any trouble when they're wronged and there are so many ways to die in their native lands that it's easy enough for them to die off without anyone asking any questions at all.

All of this for profit. The real scandal that this film was based on, involving a major drug manufacturer, is outlined in the beginning chapters of this book. As was stated, the author of the book on which the films is based said that this story is rather light compared to what really goes on in these nations, and implied that, more or less, the number of lawyers that could be involved if he said more caused him to hold back.

Enjoying this Paranoid Thriller
The conspiracy in this film is not about ideology. It's not about national security. It's not about enemies and allies, fighting an even more sinister force than the conspirators or getting revenge on someone for not toeing the military-industrial complex's line well enough. This film is about conspiracies that are based on the quest for profit.

There are several of these sorts of films in this book. *The Insider, Syriana* and *Coma* are all examples. *The Constant Gardener* is one of the finest of the lot.

This film does a great job of telling a story out of chronological order. Not only does it accomplish this rather tricky feat, but it also makes the characters incredibly engaging in doing so. The love that Tessa and Justin have for one another is believable and real. He's utterly devoted to her and, in many regards, he looks up to her. She describes seeing him as someone who represents power and authority, but who would be the first one to go out and buy fish and chips for a hungry, rioting mob if it came to that. They're both genuinely good people, and that makes them very likeable and their danger all the more visceral.

This film is complex, involves a lot of different players and doesn't resolve with a thrilling action scene. Justin and Tessa are both people who navigate the world with their ethics and their intelligence. They're not people who are warriors in the sense that they don't wield weapons or use violence well, but it's clear that they're up against people who do both.

In the end, we see Justin, a man who would have stood up for what was right, murdered by a truck full of soldiers, some of them very young.

This film is bleak, hopeless and full of despair. It doesn't give you a happy ending. Pellegrin almost certainly gets away with little more than some temporary embarrassment. This film won't make you feel good, but it will make you feel and it will make you think. *The Constant Gardener* is highly recommended for anyone who wants to see a great film with top-notch performances and an incredibly engaging plot.

Syriana (2005)

Director:

Stephen Gaghan

Starring:

Alexander Siddig

Amanda Peet

Amr Waked

Chris Cooper

Christopher Plummer

George Clooney

Jeffrey Wright

Kayvan Novak

Mark Strong

Matt Damon

Mazhar Munir

Tim Blake Nelson

William Hurt

Syriana is a complex, engaging thriller that doesn't make anything easy for the viewer, and is a better film for that fact. It centers on the oil trade, international politics and business and weaves several stories together in a way that illustrates complexity rather than provides answers.

The Plot

There are several separate plots in this film that all play out against the same backdrop of corruption, international politics and the oil trade.

The film starts out following Bob Barnes. He's a CIA field agent working in Iran. Experienced, intelligent and literate in the languages of the region, he blends seamlessly with the people he's after, arms dealers, who he means to assassinate.

Barnes brings stinger missiles to a couple of arms dealers in Iran. He makes the sale but one of the missiles is taken away by an Arab. Barnes insults the man in Farsi to verify that he doesn't speak it. As Barnes leaves the deal, the car driven by the arms dealers blows up, killing them.

Barnes starts investigating what happened and is called to a meeting of his superiors. The leader of the meeting gives him a speech about the progress the US is making in the Middle East and how it's all working out. Barnes gets angry and explains the complexity of politics in the region, insulting his superiors and making him a threat.

Barnes is sent out again to assassinate Prince Nasir, the son of an Emir and one of the few potential leaders in the Middle East who holds progressive ideals. He makes it to Lebanon and gets the okay from Hezbollah. Believing that Nasir engineered the purchase of the other missile launcher, he hires Mussawi, a killer, to help him carry out the assassination. Mussawi turns out to be working for Iran, he captures and tortures Barnes until he's interrupted by Hezbollah higher ups, who chastise Mussawi and say that Hezbollah keeps its word. Barnes gets sent back to the US.

Mussawi intends to leak the assassination plot and the CIA needs to distance itself from it. They start destroying Barnes's reputation. They cast him as a renegade agent, give him a desk job and take away his passports. Whiting, a high-ranking CIA official, is behind the setup. A friend of Barnes at the agency lets him know. Barnes engineers a meeting with Whiting and, after tolerating Whiting's faux-wisdom, explains that, if Whiting doesn't stop, Barnes will make sure Whiting and his whole family are killed. He demands his passports back and gets them.

Barnes heads back to the Middle East to prevent Nasir's assassination. Just as he gets there, however, a Predator drone launches a missile, killing Barnes, the prince and the prince's entire family.

Nasir's story plays out along with that of Woodman, an energy analyst. Woodman gets into a party held by Nasir's father in Spain. At the party, the Emir's men don't seem interested in Woodman's proposals. Later, Woodman's son is swimming in the pool when an electrical failure causes him to get electrocuted. Prince Nasir, feeling guilty for the death of Woodman's son, offers him millions in oil interests. The two gradually become close, with Woodman realizing that Nasir is quite brilliant and progressive and Nasir taking on Woodman as his economic advisor.

Nasir plans to reform his nation and their economy. He wants to take the oil wealth out of the hands of a few and use it to reform the government, wants women to have equality under the law and to otherwise modernize his nation. His father, however, wants to install his older brother as the Emir. His older brother is a spoiled imbecile of a playboy who seems likely to continue on with his father's repressive, greedy policies.

Nasir manages to get the support of several generals and becomes very popular. The CIA, recognizing that he's a threat to US business interests, engineers his assassination.

Amidst all of this are the workers in the vast Middle Eastern oil fields and we get to know one of them very well. Wasim is the son of an oil worker who is looking for work himself. A Chinese company has recently purchased the oil rights to the field where they work, putting Wasim and his father out of work and putting them both at risk of deportation. Since the company runs on a company store model, the workers are also dependent upon the company for food and housing.

Wasim tries to find work but he doesn't speak Arabic, which disqualifies him from most jobs. He goes to an Islamic school to learn Arabic—and to get food, which the school provides—and is brought into the world of radical Islamic fundamentalism. Gradually, his friend starts to become a believer in the doctrines of the Islamic school, with Wasim somewhat more hesitant, but following along as well.

The two are recruited by a fundamentalist who turns out to be the same Egyptian who took the rocket launcher at the outset of the film. Wasim and his friend are charged with piloting a small watercraft armed with the missile, which has been converted into a suicide bomb. They drive the boat into the side of an oil tanker, destroying it and killing themselves.

In the US, the storyline follows Bennett Holiday, an attorney who is working with a company called Killen, which is pursuing oil drilling rights in Kazakhstan. The company is currently merging with Connex, another oil producer. The merger is set to be approved by the government.

Holiday finds out that bribery and other corruption run to the core of the company. He finds out that one of the oilmen involved in the company, Dalton, had bribed officials in Kazakhstan. The company needs to get the Department of Justice out of their way, so Dalton is offered up as a "body" to satisfy the DOJ.

Holiday gives up Dalton but the DOJ demands more. He then sets up Sydney Hewitt, another attorney to whom Holiday is very close. He lets the CEO of Connex know about a deal that Hewitt was involved in that took advantage of his inside knowledge of the Connex-Killen merger. With Hewitt offered up to the DOJ, the merger is free to continue, creating one of the largest oil companies and economies on the planet. The film ends with Bennett returning home to find his father, an alcoholic, sitting on his stoop. He lets his father in, the POV suggesting that someone is watching from across the street.

What Real Conspiracies Look Like

In many of the films in this book there is a big reveal, usually accompanied by an information dump, where the entire conspiracy is outlined for the viewer. This is most notably—and effectively—done in *JFK*, when Donald Sutherland's old intelligence agent character lays out everything for Garrison in a string of dates, events and connections. This film doesn't do that at all and it's excellent because of it.

There are so many players, so many interests and so many different conspiracies involved in this plot that there's no moment of truth when the viewer is informed of everything. The entire affair is murky. Barnes and Prince Nasir are the characters who seem to understand the Middle East the best. Barnes may be an outsider, but he knows the players and their real motivations in the region enough to give him an edge. Nasir understands how corruption has ruined his nation and its prospects and wants to change it.

Woodman is an earnest character who really does seem to care about the Middle East at some level. In one scene, he chastises the prince for spending enormous sums of money on nothing, explaining that's just what the people in power want, for the Middle East to squander the most valuable commodity in history on greed and indulgence for a few. Nasir takes Woodman back to a private room and reveals himself in full. He's been educated in England in the US, holding a Ph.D., no less. He's intelligent, forward thinking and concerned about his people. In one scene before his assassination, his motorcade of very expensive SUVs is held up by goatherds and their large herd of goats. The prince says with some pride that the Bedouin always have the right of way and shows an obvious connection to his roots; a man who is both grounded and capable of reaching for more, and of seeing that there is more to the world than increasing his own wealth and power. Of course, this makes him a target, because people like the heads of Connex-Killen have to make a buck and Nasir threatens that.

Connex-Killen is set up as the real American interest that drives policy in the Middle East, and much of what men like Barnes are tasked with doing. One scene in this film, where Dalton gives a speech about the value of corruption, rivals the corporate speech in *Network* in terms of being a bone-chilling breakdown of both the arrogance of the people running the world's various economies—and economic scams—and the tremendous amount of power they wield. The amount of manipulation, backstabbing, corruption and smug self-satisfaction in the Connex-Killen story is nausea-inducing, but sadly believable.

Meanwhile, in the Middle East, the people at the lowest levels of society, though they may be divorced from the politics and business elements of all of this, end up paying the ultimate price. Wasim, who only wants to make some kind of a living, gets seduced by the message of Islamic extremists. An outsider from the beginning of the film, he finds that he fits in well with them as long as he falls for their lunatic politics and regressive social views. These are the men that people like Nasir were fighting against. In the end, Wasim's death is clearly personally significant, but really cannot make much of a difference in the overall outcome of all the conspiring going on in this film. His pathetically small fishing boat/bomb, dependent on oil to power its motor and using an American-made explosive device as its deadly payload, tends to emphasize this.

In the end, nothing here is really revealed. We're caught up with people of varying levels of importance in something that goes way above their heads as much as it does ours. It's a different kind of paranoid thriller, and you're going to have to let go of some of your expectations to really see this film for how good it is.

Just Watch

Roger Ebert pointed out in his review of this film that *Syriana* is not necessarily made better if one understands the characters and the many plots to a greater depth. This film is about things happening and the people involved in them, but it's all so complex that just about every viewer is going to get lost at some point. That's a strength of this film, rather than a weakness.

This film is about huge machinations launched by the most powerful economies, companies and political groups in the world. In fact, at one point, we're told straight out that the new oil company resulting from the merger of Connex and Killen is going to be among the world's largest economies. This conspiracy is bigger than any of the others in this film. It's bigger than the fake WMD intelligence in *Green Zone*, as the oil economy can be sustained for a very long time, while the Iraq War was, by design, a time-limited affair and one that's implied to play into the type of shady dealing we see here.

This film does concentrate on people from time to time, but they live in a world where virtue is the ultimate vice and where the wages of that vice are paid quickly. Nasir, a good man with a sincere desire to make his nation prosperous, is obviously not long for this world. This man respects his nation, his culture, its people and knows that his power can be used to bring great good to all in his kingdom, but none of those goals or notions serve the desires of oil companies or governments. The CIA, at one point in this film, is shown to be headed by people who mention a business friendly climate being as important as any other reform a repressive nation can take on, perhaps the most important.

The fundamentalist clerics, the sleazy oil men, the corrupt attorneys; they all get rich off of what we see going on in this film. This is their conspiracy. People like Nasir, Woodman and Barnes are interested in something bigger than profit margins, mergers, oil pipelines and the rest of it, but they also don't seem to realize that, noble as their ideals are, they're no match for the tremendous political power, money and corruption they're pitted against.

This is a confusing film, and one that is as dark as an oil slick in every regard.

Enjoying this Paranoid Thriller

From watching and reading about many of the films in this book, you'll find that even some of the best of them are rather formulaic. The protagonist gets a notion that a conspiracy is afoot, gets too close to it and puts himself or herself at risk, almost gets killed but manages to do something about it in the end, even if it's a small victory. This film is none of those things.

There's no clear main character in this film. That can easily ruin a film, but it works here. The film wanders from plot to plot but, along with the viewer, the corruption underneath every event in this film follows from scene to scene. It's the one constant. Even when the best characters—Nasir, Woodman, and Barnes—are involved, they're close to corruption and being affected by it.

The most disturbing scenes are likely those that feature the oilmen. They're ignorant, elitist, smug and arrogant. They have no idea what they're doing to the world and one strongly gets the impression that they don't care, as long as they can have conventions where they celebrate their own greatness and have more money than anyone could possibly spend in a lifetime. Watching Holiday get further and further into their world is enraging. By the end of everything, it's apparent that the merger and all of the oil companies' other interests are protected to an extent that they cannot fail. To use a term that's become popular these days, the oil companies are simply too big to fail and the US government, even down to its clandestine services, is more interested in keeping them happy than anything else.

This is a powerful, disturbing and well-made film. The performances are excellent. Oddly enough, though it is full of what might be considered politically charged material, it doesn't come off as particularly political. None of the conspiracies here imply that some people are innately good or bad. It's about power. Nadir embodies every romantic notion of the wise, powerful and just leader. The oil company execs, however, probably reflect the reality of it more accurately. Meanwhile, characters like Barnes, Holiday, Wasim and Woodman try their best to make a difference, sometimes following misguided and corrupt leaders, but are far too insignificant to make a difference.

In *Syriana*, the conspiracy isn't hidden at all. It's just too complex and powerful to be opposed and, therefore, it wins out, every time and in every situation. This film is well worth watching when you want something serious, thoughtful and thought provoking. No matter what your political beliefs may be, this film will challenge them and in the best, most intelligent way.

The International (2009)

Director:

Tom Tykwer

Starring:

Clive Owen

Naomi Watts

A very modern paranoid thriller, *The international* follows two protagonists, an Interpol operative and an American attorney as they delve into the dark world of international banks, arms deals and assassinations. This is a smart, savvy thriller that should appeal to those who want something to think about in the films that they watch, but who also appreciate some incredibly well rendered action scenes.

The Plot
The antagonist organization in this film is the International Bank of Business and Credit (IBBC), which caught the attention of an Interpol agent named Lois Salinger and an Assistant DA from New York, Eleanor Whitman. The two have been working together to investigate the bank's activities, which include arms dealing, money laundering, terrorism and assassinations.

At the beginning of the film, a whistle blower meets with a colleague of Salinger's and is promptly assassinated in broad daylight, the hit made to look like a heart attack.

The IBBC assassinates an Italian politician who is caught up in their arms deals. A patsy is arranged by the bank, who is then eliminated by a corrupt police officer. As the protagonists start to figure out who the real assassin is, they're booted out of the country by the same police officer who killed the patsy.

The investigation goes to NYC, where Saligner and Whitman get a photo of the assassin from a security camera. The assassin has a leg brace and they use it to track him down, locating the doctor who provided the brace for the assassin.

The IBBC chairman, Skarssen, details the plot to kill the Italian politician. It was to clear the way to work with his son so that they could purchase missile guidance systems, in which the bank has a financial interest. The bank now recognizes Salinger as a threat and wants to kill him.

Salinger manages to track down the assassin at the Guggenheim. Before he can get all the information he wants, however, they're attacked by hitmen working for the bank. The assassin tells Salinger that they're there for him, but that they'll kill them both. Salinger and the assassin shoot it out with the hitmen in the museum, expending round after round of ammunition as they work their way down the spiraling architecture of the building.

The assassin gets killed, but Salinger survives.

Salinger next interrogates a man named Wexler, who was a handler for the assassin. Wexler worked for the Stasi under the communist government and was, by all accounts, dedicated to the cause. He tells Salinger that the IBBC is untouchable. He also explains that, even if the IBBC was to get caught out in its illegal activities, it would only be replaced by another corrupt bank that would perform the same services for the governments, terrorists and other clients looking to work in the grey areas of the law.

Wexler tells Salinger that, if he wants to deal with the IBBC, he's going to have to go outside the law himself. Wexler also offers his assistance.

Saligner gets to the Calvini brothers, the sons of the assassinated Italian politician, and lets them know that the bank was behind the murder. In retaliation, the brothers cancel their dealings with the IBBC and order a hit on White, one of the higher-ups in the bank.

The action then goes to Istanbul. Skarssen is working out the arms deal and Salinger tries to get it on tape. He's foiled by security guards, but eventually has a standoff with Skarssen on the roofs over the streets of the city. Salinger seems ready to kill Skarssen, but a hitman shows up and kills the banker before Salinger shoots. He thanks Salinger and walks away.

The end of the film shows a US Congressional investigation kicking off into the bank, with Whitman leading the probe.

Very Intelligent

This film has some incredible dialogue in it that speaks to how conspiracies are launched and how they manage to be successful. When being interrogated by Salinger, Wexler is confronted with information from his past that makes his present life seem odd. He was once utterly devoted to the cause of communism and now works in one of the most capitalist of all sectors. Wexler dryly points out that the difference between truth and fiction is that fiction has to make sense.

This film doesn't shy away from the procedural element of the investigation and allows the viewer to see the various layers of corruption pulled away. It hints at something much bigger than what the audience gets to see at the same time. The organizations that use the IBBC's services include governments and other very powerful entities that operate outside the scope of the law. They don't just short sell stocks or sell lousy investment products to investors, these clients destabilize entire governments.

Frighteningly enough, the story in *The International* was based on real events. BCCI, the Bank of Credit and Commerce International, was found to have been involved in massive financial crimes, including money laundering, in the 1980s. It was determined to have been a racket from the start, according to the UK and US investigations into it, having been set up from the start to stay free of regulation and to do business in bank secrecy jurisdictions. Other real life crimes played into the story in this film as well.

The Shootout

This might be an intelligent thriller, but that doesn't mean that it can't have great action sequences in it. *The International* has one of the best shootout sequences of any film featured in this book.

The sequence takes place at the Guggenheim. A full-size replica of the museum was built to shoot the scene, and the filmmakers maximized their use of the environment. The gunfight winds down the museum's spiral ramp, with the participants firing an astounding amount of rounds as they battle it out. It's one of the sequences in this film that is very hard to forget and that lives up to its reputation.

The assassins and Salinger both have a very professional demeanor to them. Everyone in this movie seems intelligent and just very good at what they do. This comes through in this sequence, which avoids setting up a bunch of goons for the hero to cut through. The hitmen seem very competent at what they do, quite willing to risk being caught in the process of completing their jobs and well equipped.

There's real tension in this shootout sequence, and it helps to keep the film in the thriller mood rather than turning it into a pure action flick, even for a moment. One never gets the sense that Salinger's survival, or anyone else's, is guaranteed.

Enjoying this Paranoid Thriller
The International is a smart, classy thriller with memorable characters. The conspiracy is timely but, then again, corruption in the financial sector is always a timely topic. This film works off the connections between international politics and finance. While banks and other major financial interests are put at the center of the conspiracies in many other paranoid thrillers, *The International*, true to its name, makes apparent how massive these crimes are in scale by showing the action taking place across so many different nations. The people behind these schemes do business everywhere and with everyone. It does bring to mind the fact that, whenever there are major arms scandals, political scandals or other types of scandals, there's usually a lot of money involved at some level. Someone must be moving that money around.

While politics is said to make strange bedfellows, this film explores how finance can have the same effect. The old communist true believer, when he explains that fiction has to make sense but truth doesn't, is a great example of this.

This film has a cynical edge to it that adds to the overall dark tone. However successful the protagonists are in uncovering this conspiracy, someone else will just rise up to take the place of the IBBC. There's too much money to be made and too many interests involved for it not to happen.

The International will appeal to those who like complex plots, very timely stories and intelligent protagonists. For those who prefer more action-oriented films, the shootout at the museum in this film will make any parts you might find slower worth it. There are other great action sequences in this film as well.

Green Zone (2010)

Director:

Paul Greengrass

Starring:

Amy Ryan

Brendan Gleeson

Greg Kinnear

Jason Isaacs

Khalid Abdalla

Matt Damon

Green Zone is a paranoid thriller set during the invasion of Iraq. It tells the story of Chief Warrant Officer Roy Miller as he tracks down the source of bad intelligence on weapons of mass destruction and comes up against a conspiracy designed to keep the truth about faked intelligence a secret.

The Plot
The film opens up following General Al-Rawi, a high-ranking official in Saddam Hussein's military, as he flees during the bombing of Iraq. News reports talk about "shock and awe", a propaganda term used at the time to describe the bombing. The general knows that the regime is not going to remain in power and considers how he can ally with the Americans to keep Iraq from plunging into utter chaos and becoming a battleground

rife with foreign insurgents.

The action then picks up months later, when Chief Warrant Officer Roy Miller and his squad of US Army soldiers are hunting for weapons of mass destruction. They risk their lives to get into a warehouse that was supposed to have been secured by the time they got there, but that most certainly is not. Fighting their way into the warehouse, they find that it contains nothing except for abandoned factory equipment, which looks to have gone unused for a very long time. This marks the third time his squad has been sent out to find WMD and has come up empty handed.

Miller attends a briefing where he's given yet more information about WMD that his squad is supposed to hunt down. He questions the veracity of the intelligence and brings up the fact that every single bit of intelligence his squad has been given has turned out to be false. He questions where the intelligence comes from and is told that it's vetted, current and accurate.

A high-ranking officer listens to Miller's concerns, but then tells him to go along with the program and Miller agrees to do his job.

However, a man at the back of the briefing room turns out to be a CIA operative, Martin Brown. Brown tells Miller that his suspicions are true and that the mission Miller is being sent on is another dead end and, in fact, that the site has already been inspected and cleared as having no WMD.

The alleged source of the information is a man code-named Magellan. Magellan, however, is not available, as a WSJ reporter, Lawrie Dayne, finds out when she asks Clark Poundstone, a Pentagon official, to meet with him. Poundstone dismisses her worries that the intelligence is not good. Dayne has already published several stories touting the government's line.

Miller goes out on his next assignment. While he's there, his men detain an Iraqi who claims to have information. The man, who goes by the name Freddie, says that he saw high-ranking officials from the Ba'ath Party meeting at a house. Miller commandeers a couple of local vehicles so as not to alert the party members that they're coming and takes off with Freddie to investigate.

At the house, Miller and his men capture some of the Iraqis who are leaving. They then raid the house. They get into a fire-fight with some of the fleeing men, one of them being shot. Al-Rawi, the Jack of Clubs in the deck of cards given to US soldiers to help them identify wanted men, was at the house and Miller gets a clear view of him before Al-Rawi escapes.

One of the Ba'athists is captured and taken into custody. Miller goes to interrogate him when a Special Forces detachment shows up. Miller gets a notebook from the prisoner. The Special Forces operatives attempt to take it from him, easily best-ing Miller in a fistfight before determining that he doesn't have it and taking off.

Miller goes to the Green Zone to meet with Brown. While the streets outside are quickly becoming pandemonium, VIPs lounge poolside in one of the old palaces. Miller drops the notebook off with Brown. Brown tells Miller that he'll call and get a transfer so that Miller can start working for him. Miller runs into Dayne at the pool, who starts pressing him with ques-tions about the WMD. Miller hints that he thinks something may be wrong, and that he'll think about keeping in touch with Dayne.

Miller locates the man the Special Forces troops took and talks to him. The man is badly beaten, having been tortured. He tells Miller about a meeting that took place in Jordan and implies that they had some kind of arrangement with the US, which they'd kept.

Miller keeps investigating, finding out that Al-Rawi was the source, that Al-Rawi was giving Poundstone information, and that the Special Forces squad is working for Poundstone. They're trying to kill Al-Rawi.

This sets off a race to find the man, with Poundstone on one side and Miller and Brown on the other. Poundstone gets a hold of the notebook, which contains the information he needs to locate Al-Rawi. Miller is already off to find Al-Rawi first. Unbeknownst to Miller, Poundstone makes an announcement that all of Iraq's military and paramilitary forces have been disbanded. Miller's squad finds Al-Rawi, but Miller gets kidnapped. The military starts searching for him immediately, locating the car that took him. The Special Forces squad working for Poundstone moves in to intercept.

Miller brings up the WMD intelligence and Al-Rawi says flatly that there aren't any in Iraq and that there haven't been since the end of the first Gulf War. He was Poundstone's contact, but had not given Poundstone any intelligence saying that there was a WMD program in Iraq.

It was all fabricated. Poundstone fabricated it as part of a larger program to justify invading Iraq. Al-Rawi orders that Miller be killed and flees as the US forces start assaulting the safe house. Miller fights with the guard and gets the man's gun away. He takes off after Al-Rawi.

The Special Forces squad and Miller both race through Baghdad after Al-Rawi and one of his men. After the chasing heli-copter is shot down, Miller and one of the Special Forces oper-atives catch up. The special ops member moves to kill Al-Rawi, but gets shot down. Miller ends up holding Al-Rawi at gunpoint, but Freddie shows up and kills Al-Rawi.

Miller asks why he did it and Freddie says it's not up to Miller what happens in Iraq. Miller lets Freddie go.

Miller types up a report, leaving nothing out. He runs into Poundstone and gets into an argument with him over the rea-sons the war started. Poundstone says it doesn't matter; the two nearly get into a fight. Miller leaks his report to several news agencies along with sending a copy to Dayne.

Politically Charged

Unlike the JFK assassination or Watergate, the Iraq war is very recent. The content in this film is more politically charged simply because it deals with issues that are still currently con-tentious.

The film centers on the intelligence regarding weapons of mass destruction and their development that was used as the justifi-cation for invading Iraq in 2003. The film is told from a partic-ular angle and the director has made no secret of that. It's well documented that false statements were made by the highest level officials in the lead up to war, and that those statements were known to be false at the time they were made. This film is built on that.

It's also built on a sort of conspiracy of complicity on the part of the media. The reporter character, Dayne, can really repre-sent any news agency that fell for the phony intelligence. Dayne is obviously catching on to the fact that she was lied to.

Poundstone is the total liar. He's cynical and nihilistic to the core. He wanted war, for any reason, whether that reason was true or false and felt that the righteousness of the plan superseded the requirement for truth. He's an ugly character and his Special Forces detachment is very much a dark contrast to Miller and his squad, who are driven to do what they do for all the right reasons.

This is a very politically charged film and it did raise its fair share of controversy at the time. Agree with it or not, however, this film really is a well-made conspiracy thriller. Whether the political message makes you bristle or makes you cheer, the way this film is constructed is very good.

The Paranoid Thriller Core

Good paranoid thrillers need a likeable and curious protagonist with a lot of courage to back up their convictions. They also need some sort of a very powerful force for that protagonist to be pitted against. To make it really work, there has to be a sense that the protagonist could fail in their mission. Happy endings are not guaranteed in this genre, which is one of the things that really make it great.

This film gives all of this and more. Miller is a great character. He's pretty much what everyone who identifies soldiering with an expression of sacrifice and honor has in mind. He believes in his mission, he's good at what he does and he's not afraid to question authority if it happens to be wrong about something.

His CIA contact, Brown, is probably what people hope CIA agents are like. He's smart, a chess player type, who understands all the pieces on the board, how they interact and how to use them to get to a desired goal. He's not inhuman, however, and seems to have a bit of professional pride. He seems genuinely offended by the incompetence he sees around him, and even more so by the arrogance that goes along with it in people like Poundstone.

Poundstone is a psychopath. He doesn't see war as a tragedy, but a tool. He also doesn't seem to understand when he's losing. Baghdad is burning and becoming increasingly violent while he struts around inside the Green Zone. In most every scene, he has the air of someone who feels like they know just a bit more than everyone around them, though he's deeply unqualified for the amount of power that he wields. He's dishonest to the core and clearly sees people as things to be manipulated and, when they're inconvenient, executed.

As is the case with any conspiracy thriller, the worst people are always the insiders with the most access to power. Miller's hand-to-hand tussle with the special ops solider sums that up. The people Miller is butting heads with are simply better at what they do and more powerful than him. He's outclassed by them, but he's also determined not to let that stop him from getting to the truth.

The action sequences in this film are remarkably well done. They're fast-paced and very intense. They're also used incredibly as metaphors. When the Iraqi military higher-ups flee from the US soldiers, they run through the landscape as only people who truly understand it in every regard can. When they barge through a door, they simply call out to the families in the homes and they're allowed through quickly, even assisted in some regards. When the US soldiers come through in pursuit, they're distracted, resisted and obviously outsiders.

The US has incredible technology on display in this film. They can track a car instantly and get constant position information on their target and themselves in real time. The Iraqi soldiers and fighters need none of this, so the scenes are kept from falling into dunderheaded action sequences. There's a sense of danger during all of these sequences and the shooting style is frantic at times.

Enjoying this Paranoid Thriller

Green Zone really has a lot to offer as a conspiracy, paranoid thriller. It moves along quickly and is very much a modern film. It provides an action sequence right after the opening, so there isn't a long setup. This is a very modern film in that regards. It never stops or really slows down much at all.

The film gives an interesting twist in making both the problem and the good guy part of the military-industrial complex. Not only that, but they're both really looking out for the interests of the military-industrial complex.

Miller and Brown both take pride in what they do. They seem driven to be serving a higher purpose than themselves or their own ideals and can't let go of the fact that something is obviously very wrong with what's going on around them. This makes them very likeable.

Somewhere in the middle ground is Dayne, the reporter. She's been duped and, to demonstrate just how poor her reporting skills are, she goes looking to a CIA agent and a military source for more information. The media in this film, as represented through her, seem utterly dependent upon other people to do their jobs, and really haven't much to them at all.

Poundstone and his crew are definitely on the dark side of things here and they're formidable. They're much scarier than anyone else in the film, in fact. Our protagonist, though he's portrayed by the same actor, is no Jason Bourne. He's an average solider who's gotten disgruntled. Poundstone and his Special Forces squad are professionals and, at least as far as burying the truth is concerned, if nothing else, they know what they're doing.

The action sequences do not leave the viewer wanting. They're graphic, brutal and filled with confusion, but not in the sense that it's hard to follow the action. This film doesn't substitute fast editing and senseless shots for good action sequences. You have a sense of where the characters are, what's going on around them and where the danger is, and that makes these sequences very engaging on the whole.

The political theme of this thriller may put some people off, but it's worth seeing. The film does what a paranoid thriller should. It introduces a complex, powerful force and lets us figure out what it really is going on with the protagonist. There's a lot of danger along the way. This film definitely falls into the action thriller category, so that danger doesn't come in the form of sinister phone calls, veiled threats and so forth. It comes out of a gun and is delivered by some very intimidating people.

The film has great production values and performances are strong all round. It also provides a modern installment of the paranoid thriller genre that addresses contemporary issues. These films really had a surge in popularity in the 1970s, so newer ones offer something a bit different and, for some people, the tension might be more engrossing when the conspiracy surrounds more recent stories than Watergate or JFK.

Green Zone is definitely worth seeing, particularly if you want a bit more action than the average paranoid thriller offers.

http://www.theguardian.com/film/2010/mar/08/paul-greengrass-betrayal-green-zone

http://www.washingtonsblog.com/2009/11/everyone-knew-that-iraq-didnt-have-wmds.html

Further Recommendations

If you liked the films in this book, you'll likely find these enjoyable as well. Some of them are so well known that they didn't get included in the second section, with plenty of information on them being available already.

The 39 Steps (1935)

This film was remade in the 1950s, but the original version is directed by Hitchcock and, thus, well worth seeing. The story follows a man who gets involved with international espionage and who has to flee for his life and for his freedom as he's framed for murder.

The Manchurian Candidate (1962)

Frank Sinatra stars in this film detailing a communist conspiracy to assassinate American political figures. Mind control, sleeper agents and other conspiracy standards are all among the sinister elements of the plot. This pre-Watergate thriller harkens back to the days when the worst threats to the American way of life—at least in American films—was regarded as coming from without, rather than within the power structure itself.

The Odessa File (1974)

A sinister organization of former SS officers called ODESSA is at the heart of this film's dark narrative. A reporter is determined to track down a Nazi war criminal and tries to get into an organization that keeps them safe from detection and prosecution. In doing so, he also discovers that the SS officer he's after is still in the warmongering business and that the organization that protects him is both powerful and deadly.

All the President's Men (1976)

This is widely considered to be one of the best films of its era. It follows Bob Woodward and Carl Bernstein as they start to unravel the Watergate conspiracy, to which many of the films in this book owe significant parts of their plotlines. This is the real deal. If you didn't learn them from the book or the actual reporting, this is where terms like "Deep Throat" and conspiracy-busting wisdom such as "follow the money" came into the public consciousness. This is an intense film and an absolute must-see for anyone who wants a deeper understanding of the paranoid political thrillers of the 70s and even those of the present day.

Silkwood (1983)

Dark and intense, this film follows Karen Silkwood as she tries to take on a nuclear power company. When the company starts putting the lives of its workers at risk to keep profits high, Karen finds herself at the center of a controversy that threatens very powerful interests. This film doesn't make any conclusions about the real life events it's based on, but it certainly makes some strong suggestions.

Conclusion

The tone of paranoid thrillers has remained remarkably consistent over the years. The nature of being paranoid, of course, does not really change much. The nature of what makes one paranoid, however, very much does.

Through the decades that the films featured in this book span, you'll see a marked shift in the conspiracies that provide the antagonists. In the earlier films, the threats are oftentimes foreign nations or outside entities trying to take over free nations. Assassinations are carried out by one or two powerful people backed by lackeys of various sorts, such as in *The Man Who Knew Too Much.*

After Watergate and Kennedy's assassination, however, the conspiracies go through a significant transformation. We have films like *The Parallax View*, which serves as a way of relating a conspiracy theory about the Kennedy assassination. A special company designed to back up the interests of the military-industrial complex through targeted assassinations is to blame. *Three Days of the Condor* plays on Watergate style conspiracy, with clandestine agencies withholding vital information from the public and private heavies doing the dirty work of keeping lose ends under control.

Corporate conspiracies come into play later, with films like *Coma* showing the horrible nexus of unaccountable power and the desire to make a buck no matter what the real cost.

Films that involved Nazi conspiracies were very popular in the 1970s, but have almost dropped off the map, for obvious reasons. In the end, some of those war criminals may have managed to flee and live out their lives never being held accountable for what they did, but no one can hide from time. Films such as *The Boys from Brazil*, however, imply that those criminals may have found ways to preserve their awful legacy, and invoke an entirely other type of paranoia.

The most recent paranoid thrillers in this book stay close to current events, for the most part. *Green Zone* references the intelligence that led to the Iraq war; *The International* involves financial sector corruption; *The Insider* is based on a real-life incident of corporations conspiring to hide damaging information from the public.

Then there are those films in this book that concentrate on conspiracies to manipulate perception. *Capricorn One, Blow Out, and JFK*: these films all involve plots where very powerful interests conspire to change the public perception of reality, and they oftentimes succeed. Of all of them, *JFK* is the finest example and is definitely worth seeing more than once, simply because of the complex tangle of interests and actions it lays out.

No matter when they were made, however, paranoid thrillers almost always feature one person or a group of people fighting hard against an unaccountable, deadly and powerful conspiracy that tries to take something away from society without society catching on. What they take away might be the peace that a new president might contribute to bringing about; it might be the safety of knowing that your doctor or pharmaceutical company works within ethical and transparent guidelines; or it might simply be the notion that, whatever your government might be up to, it's got your best interests in mind.

In these films, none of those notions are true. There's always some dark operator behind the scenes, some story that sounds like a conspiracy theory but isn't and a lot of power-hungry people pulling the strings on all of it.

These films might play on conspiracy theory themes, but keep in mind that many of them are based in reality. Some of them, like *Enemy of the State*, have eerily predicted how events actually unfolded long after they were made.

Sometimes, conspiracy theories are just paranoia, in other cases they are just a pastime that people like to enjoy. Sometimes, they're based in something real, but stretched to the point that, in the end, they're nearly all speculative.

Then again, sometimes we find out that the NSA really is monitoring everyone's communications, that they've been doing it for some time and that they even misled the public about what they were up to. Sometimes corporations do lie, such as in the case of the tobacco companies.

Sometimes, paranoid people are just the people who figure it out first—and often those people pay the highest price of all for exposing it to the world.

Sources Cited:

http://www.npr.org/2014/04/16/303733011/edward-snowden-from-geeky-drop-out-to-nsa-leaker

http://www.cnn.com/2003/US/03/14/sprj.irq.documents/

http://forums.randi.org/archive/index.php/t-151294.html

http://www.pbs.org/wgbh/pages/frontline/shows/reaction/interact/silkwood.html

http://watergate.info/

http://www.marketwatch.com/story/enron-caused-california-blackouts-traders-say

http://www.ushmm.org/wlc/en/article.php?ModuleId=10007060

http://edition.cnn.com/2006/US/06/06/nazi.crimes/

http://news.nationalgeographic.com/news/2013/13/130507-nazi-war-criminal-holocaust-auschwitz-hans-lipschis-simon-wiesenthal-center-demjanjuk/

http://www.disclose.tv/

http://www.history.com/shows/ancient-aliens

http://tvtropes.org/pmwiki/pmwiki.php/Main/Infodump

http://www.usatoday.com/story/news/nation-now/2013/11/21/john-kennedy-conspiracy-theories-assasination/3661891/

https://www.youtube.com/watch?v=iRN0GDFH3Vs

http://www.weather.com/health/just-prick-origin-and-evolution-anti-vaccine-movement-20140228

http://www.vanityfair.com/magazine/archive/1996/05/wigand199605

http://www.bloomberg.com/news/2014-01-10/tobacco-companies-u-s-agree-on-ads-admitting-smoking-lies-1-.html

http://www.reuters.com/article/2013/08/05/us-dea-sod-idUSBRE97409R20130805

http://en.wikipedia.org/wiki/Simon_Wiesenthal

http://www.rottentomatoes.com/m/1002993-boys_from_brazil/

http://www.chicagoreader.com/chicago/the-boys-from-brazil/Film?oid=1067224

https://www.princeton.edu/~achaney/tmve/wiki100k/docs/Project_MKULTRA.html

http://educate-yourself.org/nwo/reportironmountain1.shtml

http://mcadams.posc.mu.edu/sbt.htm

http://mcadams.posc.mu.edu/back.jpg

http://mcadams.posc.mu.edu/jimloon5.htm

http://www.aarclibrary.org/publib/jfk/arrb/report/html/arrb_fin_027.htm

http://www.washingtonpost.com/opinions/woodward-and-bernstein-40-years-after-watergate-nixon-was-far-worse-than-we-thought/2012/06/08/gJQAlsi0NV_story.html

http://www.archives.gov/research/jfk/warren-commission-report/

http://www.jta.org/2013/08/22/news-opinion/politics/new-nixon-tapes-show-more-anti-semitism

http://www.history.com/topics/energy-crisis

http://www.rogerebert.com/scanners/the-critics-were-horrified-4-undervalued-scary-movies-on-dvd

http://www.rottentomatoes.com/m/they_live/

http://tvtropes.org/pmwiki/pmwiki.php/Main/ImperialStormtrooperMarksmanshipAcademy

https://www.youtube.com/watch?v=EU-IBF8nwSY

http://articles.chicagotribune.com/1988-11-07/features/8802130777_1_john-carpenter-aliens-enlightenment

http://tvtropes.org/pmwiki/pmwiki.php/Film/TheyLive

http://www.skepdic.com/subliminal.html

http://www.newscientist.com/special/unbreakable-codes

http://www.pro-technix.com/information/crypto/pages/vernam_base.html

https://archive.org/details/ird059

http://www.cbsnews.com/news/claim-lecarres-the-constant-gardener-was-based-on-pfizer-trovan-case/

http://knowfuture.wordpress.com/2007/07/09/pfizers-trovan-outrage-in-nigeria-on-film-dying-for-drugs/

http://www.rogerebert.com/reviews/syriana-2005

http://www.nationaljournal.com/tech/edward-snowden-nsa-spies-more-on-americans-than-russians-20140430

http://www.theguardian.com/world/edward-snowden

http://www.theguardian.com/world/2013/jun/06/nsa-phone-records-verizon-court-order

http://www.washingtonpost.com/blogs/the-switch/wp/2014/01/27/darrell-issa-james-clapper-lied-to-congress-about-nsa-and-should-be-fired/

http://www.latimes.com/world/worldnow/la-fg-wn-obama-nsa-spying-chinese-president-20140324,0,3780214.story#axzz30Oxavsm4

http://www.nytimes.com/2007/10/14/opinion/14sun1.html?pagewanted=print&_r=0

http://www.nytimes.com/1999/11/03/arts/tv-notes-mike-wallace-getting-over-it.html?pagewanted=all&src=pm

http://en.wikipedia.org/wiki/Bank_of_Credit_and_Commerce_International

http://www.firstshowing.net/2009/behind-the-scenes-video-of-
the-guggenheim-shootout-in-the-international/

Made in the USA
Las Vegas, NV
25 August 2021